TWO MATADORS

---

a novella by

MARCUS MCGEE

PEGASUS BOOKS

Pegasus Books
3338 San Marino Avenue
San Jose, CA 95127
www.pegasusbooks.net

First Edition: April 2012

Published in North America by Pegasus Books. For information, please contact Pegasus Books c/o Caprice De Luca, 3338 San Marino Avenue, San Jose, CA 95127.

Library of Congress Cataloguing-In-Publication Data
McGee, Marcus
Two Matadors/Marcus McGee – 1st edition
     p. cm.
Library of Congress Control Number: 2012935395
ISBN - 978-0-9832608-9-9

1. Drama: Continental European. 2. History : Europe - Spain & Portugal. 3. Family & Relationships : Love & Romance. 4. Body, Mind & Spirit : Spirituality - Course in Miracles.

10 9 8 7 6 5 4 3 2

Comments about *Two Matadors* and requests for additional copies, book club rates and author speaking appearances may be addressed to Pegasus Books or to Caprice De Luca at cdeluca@pegasusbooks.net or you can send your comments and requests via e-mail to mmcgee@pegasusbooks.net.

Also available as an eBook from Internet retailers and from Pegasus Books

Printed in the United States of America

This for the heart she fills with profound lust
This for the passion fate will not deny
This for the soul that I will ever trust
This for immortal love that cannot die

This for... mi propio Isabel

El amor junta los cetros con los cayados;
la grandeza con la bajeza,
hace posible lo imposible;
iguala diferentes estados
y viene a ser poderoso como la muerte.

Miguel de Cervantes

TWO MATADORS

Marcus McGee

TWO MATADORS

The Story of a Lifetime, a poetic composition

Tercio de Los Tontos

If the strained and pained words I've heard from dying men are true, then age has a way of elevating one's sense of perspective, and the resulting wisdom is tinged with a certain cynicism about the vanity of it all, which is natural. And yet for the truly fortunate, there is a subtle art or poetry to a life lived, if we stick around long enough and have both the appreciation and naïveté to understand it.

I found myself in old Sevilla, in the south of Spain, and on a quest to taste the blood of vines, the *Manzanilla, Fino, Moscatel, Oloroso* and of course, the *Amontillado*. When I had my fill, I then decided to enjoy and to explore the city—seek its history, the monuments and families, for after all, it was a city with a lurid legacy—romantic Moorish palaces, traditions, fascinating secrets whispered down for over thirteen hundred years, a sort of magic best enjoyed within a state of wine-inspired bliss.

I must admit I was inspired on the day I went to visit *La Maestranza*, possibly the grandest architectural work within the city and the oldest *Plaza de Toros* in the world, located on Baratillo Hill. I felt uneasy going in because I knew it was a plaza meant for fighting bulls and I abhorred the exploitation of all living things. And yet I got no sense of nature being out of sync. There was no hint of cruelty or meanness in the stone or sand or air, so I went in.

To my relief, no fight was scheduled for the day, providing me an opportunity to walk the weathered stairs and to admire the arena's innermost *facade*, called *El Palco del Príncipe*, its theatre box constructed to accommodate the Spanish royal family. I saw the *ochovas*, eight arches, orange with blue and white-tiled ceilings, and the marble sculptures all about the place, which were the work of artisans from Portugal. Out on the sand, I saw the ghosts of many matadors and bulls, engaged forever in the spoors of time.

As I was just about to leave that lesser wonder of the world, I saw a tiny group assembled at the center of the ring. There was an older, white-haired man who struggled forward on a rolling chair, and walking next to him, a beautiful young woman urging him until he stopped. I saw two male attendants and a small assemblage, which included six or seven withered individuals, a news reporter and a man who photographed the group.

I watched as one attendant helped the man stand from the chair beneath a pale and gloomy sky, and then the striking woman placed a sword in his vibrating hands. All held their breath and bowed as he raised heavenward the steel with tired, shaking arms, and they applauded as attendants rescued him from such a heavy blade. The ceremony done, I followed with my eyes until they reached the lower section where they came into the passageway.

As Fate would have it, I was just behind the group as they were in the corridor, and when the old man saw me, right away he rose while shouting, pointing all the while at me.

"*El Moro!*" he exclaimed, "Morisco, you are *here!*"

I understood what he was saying in the Spanish tongue, but I was sure he had to be confused, senile or drunk. Yet on the other hand, there was a certain irony, since I was *born* in Casablanca and was recently researching my Moroccan ancestry. However, ' I was an American, for all my life.

"You come as family," the feeble man insisted urgently. "You come with me! You come to tell the story of my life! A gypsy woman told me many years ago *el Moro* would arrive today."

I really hadn't come to tell his story. No, I came to southern Spain exploring earthy wines and the *flamenco*. Then again, I always had been fascinated by the story of a life, and after witnessing the solemn ritual performed out on the plaza sand, I found myself intrigued. I saw the motorcade outside the building, indicating Old World wealth. In viticulture logic, that desperate and enigmatic man would probably possess some rare, extraordinary wines. A voice within my head told me to go, and so I went to hear his story... *and to drink his wine.*

The old man said it was a house, but what I saw was more a palace, crafted in eleventh-century Moorish style. The stone exterior was ancient, with creatively carved arches, decorated painted tiles, with Arabic calligraphy and scenic garden views. I drew a breath, while savoring the peaceful and pervasive fragrance of the orange blossoms from the many trees established all about the grounds.

"And wine—the cellar by itself was larger, footage-wise, than my entire house! I had my laptop and a camera, along with my small tape recorder, so I was prepared to hear his story then, but he explained that he would share it after food and drink.

I learned his name was called Fernando Castañeda de Castilla. From the numerous portraits, honors, trophies and his accolades displayed about the residence, I gathered that he was a famous matador in his own day. And after they congratulated him, his entourage made various excuses and they left.

Sevilla is in Spain within the Andalusian region of the southern portion on the vast Iberian Peninsula. The city and its neighbors call themselves "autonomous communities." The region's contribution to the world? Outstanding wines, which I had spent the last two weeks consuming, and of course, bullfighting and *flamenco* dance.

The Moors, or *el Moriscos*, led by Tariq el Tuerto, came to Andalucía in 711 A.D. and they remained until 1212—five hundred years, while leaving in their wake great legacies in architecture, culture, food, tradition and religion, even kindred blood. The skin of the familiar, striking woman who attended me was tan, her facial features seeming subtly northern African, yet she was Sevillana. She was captivating and attractive, and she smelled of fresh spring mint. Her name was Fátima.

The stately man and I were all alone within that huge estate, save for the workers who were going here and there, and Fátima, who made my breathing thin and shallow when she came and when she went. The servants called him "Maestro." He was on a bland and soft foods diet, so his meal consisted of fermented pears and dates, *Manchego* cheese and tiny, flaky morsels of tilapia. The chef made me a steak, along with fresh green beans and *pan de Horno*. Naturally, we both were lovers of the vine.

"The very best from all my wines!" he promised me, and what we drank was absolutely marvelous, beginning with the first decanted bottle, trickled in my glass. It was a soft and subtle, satiny and rich *rioja*, ruby-colored and without a label, symbol or a *DO* status there.

"You are *El Moro* and you come to share the story of my life. Today. Right now!" he said in Spanish. "*You will see me die today!*"

"*¿El final de tu vida?*" I asked. "I do not know your life, *Señor*."

"Yet you will write!" he chided me. "I'll speak in English, you will write it down. This is my life. When I was born here in Sevilla, in this very house, I was not born alone, since twenty-seven minutes after me, my brother came. Fernando he was called. Perhaps he would have come out first or not. I do not know, but if I had to guess, then I would say he waited there. For me, I rush into all things, and yet Fernando—he was always... thinking deep and contemplating things. Fernando did not know what danger there could be outside of where we were, outside the womb, so he was paralyzed perhaps by fear or his portentous thoughts. Fernando balked, and so it was that I went first into the world."

The old man sipped the wine, his spirit on the rise.

"*Imagen del espejo gemelos idénticos!*" he said. "Yes, 'mirror image twins, identical'—that was the name for us, for what we were. Identical, but not exact—like looking in a mirror glass. Fernando's left hand was his favorite, but here—" he raised an arm. "My right always protected me."

"And I was always brave and daring, maybe sometimes reckless as a boy, but then Fernando—he was tentative and careful," he continued. "He was smart and studying all the time. Fernando had a mind for understanding hard-to-understand ideas. In many ways we were alike, but that division made us different, his way of thinking things. Our hates were similar, although our loves were twins as we were twins.

"Together, we detested Franco and the Spanish Civil War. We loved Picasso and delicious Alicante bread, but most especially, we loved *corrida de toros*—which is bullfighting," he said. "When we were little boys, our mother fashioned us small capes and we took sticks to fight against the biggest, meanest goats in all Sevilla—*el corrida de cabras* we called it while performing for Papa. Yet even then, we were the same and very different. I was the fighter with no fear who routed goats both mean and large. Fernando—he had trepidation, a foreboding sense, which caused him to retreat into the shade and safety the books, yet even then.

"So by the time we had eleven years," the maestro said, "we made announcements saying we would one day soon become world-famous matadors, and on that day, *corrida* was a passion for Fernando and for me. Then at the age of twelve, Papa sent us away to school so we could train as matadors. We traveled to Carmona, which was thirty-two kilometers away from home. We were enrolled there in a celebrated school for fighting bulls, where we were trained to imitate the Manolete style."

He closed his eyes, remembering over many years.

"Papa José, he was a matador before I was, but life was very different for him," he sighed. "His father once had wealth, though not so much to send him to a celebrated school for matadors. And so to learn he had to go from town to town to fight with bulls in very dangerous contests called *capeas*. The danger in the sport was great because the bulls were old and smart.

"Papa was called a *maletilla* in these fights, and many of his friends who also worked as *maletillas* suffered injuries or crippling in the dusty fields where *capeas* were fought, and some were killed by bulls. The greatest danger to these *maletillas* did not come from bulls. It was instead the greed and the neglect of those promoting them. Papa was gored two times when he was young, but he was fortunate. Not even one in several hundred *maletillas* ever made it to the famous plazas and a better life."

"And your papa?" I asked while still in awe within the luxurious home. "He made it to the famous plazas and a better life?"

"He was José Castañeda de Castilla," the old man stated proudly, "probably the best torero ever fighting bulls in Andalucía in his time, but he was never paid the money he deserved. Because he was not trained by teachers at a formal school, he did not know the fancy passes, and he did not have the style required for the contests sponsored by the well-to-do promoters at the festivals and matches where a matador could become rich. And for this cause, to him it was important for his sons to learn the art and style at a respected school. Where he could not instruct Fernando and myself, he saved his money so that we would learn it at the school. We were not rich, but we also were not poor. Our life was good enough."

I had to stop because I was perplexed. This man had said "Fernando" was his "*brother*" several times, and so I thought he was confused. The servants even said *he* was Fernando, which was odd.

Within the atrium, there was displayed a massive oil portrait of José, the father of Fernando and Antonio, and it was painted when José was young. He was a handsome, focused man with dark and piercing eyes. His sons no doubt were handsome also in their youth, while they aspired to be matadors.

"Because we lacked experience with horses at the time," he said, "we started at the school to be *peones*, helpers to the banderilleros, both of us."

I was intrigued to hear his explanation, but I had to ask.

"Banderilleros?" I inquired. "Why so much to fight a bull?"

"To fight a bull is to perform a miracle," he answered me. "A man alone can never win against a bull, and so it helps to have belief. The bull is far too strong and way too fast. Morisco, you recall eleven other labors tasked to Hercules, but number seven was to catch and fight a bull? Yet Hercules was represented as a demigod, whereas the matador is just an ordinary man.

"And so to fight a bull, there is no way to win except to weaken it and slow it down to give the man a fighting chance. We *all* fight bulls within our lives. The matador is just the man who faces the impossible, the *inconceivable*, and wins."

He smiled and looked at me.

"Do you believe in God?" he asked.

"This is a question that has haunted me for all my life, *Señor*," I sighed. "In answer, I do not believe, but neither do I disbelieve."

"Then you are not convinced," he shrugged. "And have you ever faced a bull?"

"I never have," I answered him.

"To face a bull means facing fear and then appreciating what inspires your belief," he said. "The bull is nature, in its most prevailing, intellectual and dangerous form. A man who has not learned to conquer fear within himself will never win a match against a bull, not even in its weakened form. At first, the matador must tame the nature in his heart in order to subdue what lies beyond."

I wrote as quickly as I could to capture how he voiced his phrases, fashioned images and used such lofty speech.

"But now I sound more like my brother, the philosopher" the old man laughed. "So tell me, do you know how much a bull can weigh? And can you comprehend its monstrous size? Morisco, have you seen a bull up close?"

"Yes, only on the television," I admitted, laughing to myself.

"A fighting bull is fourteen hundred pounds!" he sneered. "Yes, fourteen hundred pounds, and sometimes more! Eight times as big as you, four times as fast and thirty times as strong! You might be smarter when outside the ring, but in the ring, the bull is smarter than you are. And even after he is weak, a human does not stand a chance... unless there's something more *within* the man which he believes, and only that can save his soul.

"No man is able to defeat a bull alone. Perhaps a weak American bull, but not the *Toro Bravo*, not the fighting bull of Spain," he said. "In order to subdue this strong-willed bull, you must possess a team of brave men, fools and horses. More than that—the will of Fate. So when Fernando went with me to school for fighting bulls, we learned enough to be considered fools. The thought to fight a bull came from your family, Morisco. It was introduced to Spain in the eleventh century by the Moors who fought the bulls on backs of horses. Did you know that fact?"

"No," I admitted quietly.

"And have you ever watched a bullfight then, Morisco?" he inquired.

"Yes, I did when I was younger," I replied, "I did so when my family was living in Madrid. I watched the matadors on television. I did not perceive the meaning, though I watched."

"Then you have seen it is a marvel to behold," he said. "And here in Spain it is not harsher to the bull than to the man. It is a mortal drama, a decisive contest testing man and nature, played before an audience who learns important lessons from their safety in the stands.

"Not for the bull—" I said. The bull must always die."

"And *men* must die! Good men do die!" he angrily asserted, almost screaming with a passion. "Some physically within the ring, while bleeding from their outward wounds, and others die more slowly in a subtle way, and bleed from wounds within. While every man is born with something of a bull within his heart, this raging spirit in the heart can die. When this occurs, these men will never live excitement or adventure. They will never please a woman or inspire children, as they are dead within for all their lives."

He paused to take a breath and wipe his eyes.

"And even when men win against the bull, they still possess compassion they inherit from our God," he said. "A good, enlightened matador will not allow the bull to suffer agony. Men can be merciful, but bulls—there is no trace of mercy in their souls. If you have ever watched a bull destroy a person, then no longer will you feel so sorry for the bull."

He sighed and wagged his head.

"Morisco, on your face I now see such compassion for the bull, but I saw little there when you were eating beefsteak for your dinner meal," he laughed, "and as I watched you picking flesh the persecuted bull has left between your teeth. *Maroc*, the country of your birth is wonderful, but you have learned to be American by judging superficially, have learned to be a hypocrite."

I looked to tabletop to see my empty plate, with only fat and bone remaining there.

"It is 'compassionate' Americans," he said, "who will consume more beef than all the world—for years they have and will. In order to consume so much, they slaughter many bulls. In all of Spain, not more than sixty thousand die in plazas in one year, and they are used for food. But in America, six *hundred* thousand bulls are cruelly slaughtered in one week! That's more than eighty thousand in one day, three hundred sixty days per year! Again, that's eighty thousand bulls in every single day! And whether in the bullring or the slaughterhouse—the bulls must die. While in America, I made a visit to a cattle slaughterhouse, and after that experience, I've never eaten beef again. For me, it's only fish and milk and vegetation now."

I looked to view his empty plate, and I could only shrug.

"So whether at the plazas or the slaughterhouses," Maestro said, "bulls wish to live, but there they bleed and die. When in the slaughterhouse, no bull will ever have a chance to live, no single bull, no single chance. Inside the plaza, on the contrary, bulls have at least a fighting chance to win and live. And sometimes, even when the matador prevails, the bull survives. Did you know that?"

"I did not know," I answered him.

"Yes!" he affirmed. "The most strong-willed and terrifying bull I ever fought, called *el Pecado*—this untiring bull that day did fight so well and smart and without fear so that the crowd began to understand these qualities through him that day. He made them better know and understand the character within themselves. And for that he was *indultado*. So they waved the handkerchiefs and then *el presidente* pardoned this brave bull."

"What happened to him after that?" I asked.

"This *el Pecado*—pardoned, went back to the ranch and to a life of constant feeding and relentless breeding," Maestro laughed. "His life was better than my own! Like Agamemnon, I returned to understand betrayal, mine and hers, as I was stabbed and left for dead."

He paused to redirect his thoughts.

"When fools and men prepare to fight a bull," he said, "they know the bull must bleed to lessen stamina. If not, the bullfight would go on for many hours while the crowd would tire and the bull would win. So first of all, the bull must bleed. This part is *tercio de varas*, or 'the introduction to the bull.' Within this stage the *picadors* come out on horses and use lances meant to cut and weaken the *morrillo*—or the massive muscle of the neck behind the head and horns. The bull then bleeds, and it begins to tire after it attacks the padded horses, blindfolded to ease their fear. The bull attempts to lift the horses off the ground by using horns and weakened neck to only tire more."

The maestro sipped his wine again, continuing.

"Then after several years attending school in picturesque Carmona, I was, with Fernando, good enough with horses to become a picador. But first, we were the helpers to the banderilleros there.

The picadors, when after they have gone away, the banderilleros come with blue and pink *capotes*, usually beside the matador. It is their job to finally prepare the bull by placing darts with barbs within the muscles of the shoulders and the neck. This slows the bull's reflexes and it lessens its ability to hook or toss or gore. This part is *tercio de banderillas*. After that, then comes the matador.

Señor coughed violently, as old men sometimes do, and then he cleared his throat.

"The final part is *tercio de muerte*, or the third of 'death,' and this means either that the bull will die or that perhaps the matador will die. The other guys, they go out there and they harass the bull, but 'matador' means 'he who kills.' So he comes out, the red cape in one hand, the sword concealed behind muleta. Then begins the dance..."

The old man waved his hands to imitate the graceful movements of *flamenco* poetry.

"It is the dance of death," he said. "*Pase de pecho, revolera pase de desprecio, remate, revolera! ah ¡ole! mariposa, manoletina, kikiriki! ah ¡ole!* And if the matador is good, death comes both quick and clean in *estocada* at the end. The bull will suffer little and the matador is celebrated for his bravery, his art and his success at overcoming nature and himself."

"You were a famous matador?" I asked. "Your brother and yourself?"

The old man sighed in sadness as he looked into the past.

"Yes, in the end my brother as a matador in life was better than I ever was." *Señor* looked up and smiled. "The story of one lifetime I will share tonight, and you will write it down and tell it to the world, Morisco. You will tell it for all time for us. So long ago, I took my brother's life, but more about that later in the night."

He closed his eyes a moment and began.

"It was the week before our graduation to be matadors, and we were practicing within the plaza with a younger bull. He was *uno novillo*, three years old, when we were then surprised to see another bull, a larger bull, both mean and smart—a huge *Miura*, called *el Diablo* by the squires. The bull had broken out his pen and through the gate before he came onto the sand. The best friend of Fernando was a gypsy who was younger than we were and who we called Gitano. He was third of three when we were banderilleros.

"¡Ay, Dios!" *Señor* continued with a sigh. "Gitano did not see *Diablo* come. Distracted by the bull in front of him, he did not realize *Diablo* pawed the ground, prepared to charge. Diablo's body was a blur until he hooked Gitano, horn right through his back— *Diablo* lifted him and shook him with great violence, tossing him across the ring. All bleeding, wounded, on the ground, Gitano was no match for such an angry bull. His body flew from place to place, a straw within the whirling wind. *Diablo*, fire in his eyes, attacked again with horns, with hooves, and always with his heart."

The maestro raised a hand and patted three times at his heart.

"And after all the time and bravery it took to get the bull away from him, Gitano lay there, covered all with blood that gushed from many wounds. His face was crushed, and his intestines trailed outside his body, staining red the plaza sand. It was an awful sight, a vision that will never leave my mind. Because he was Fernando's favorite friend, my brother took it worse with his foreboding sense. He left the plaza on that day, so he did not become a matador."

"You said he *was* a matador," I said, correcting him. "You said your brother as a matador was better than you ever were!"

"I did. Fernando left the ring that day and never finished at the school," *Señor* explained. "I did not know until my father's funeral where he had gone, and when I saw him, he was older and more handsome after so much time, but still he looked like me. So I was handsome too, of course." The old man drank and crossed his arms.

"Fernando left the ring, and then he went to college at *La Universidad de Sevilla*, where he studied physiology, veterinary science and zoology. Then he became professor there, a teacher of philosophy and the *Tauromaquia*. For seven years I did not see Fernando, though I loved him all that time. Then at my father's funeral, two mirror-image brothers, two companions of the womb—these two who loved so much began to bear a bitter hate."

"Now let me guess," I interjected. "Tragically, there was a girl?"

"Of course there was a girl! In any story worth remembering, there *always* is a girl," he nodded, laughing to himself. "The name that she was called was Isabella Castañeda de Zamora—she was more than just a girl. She was a splendid flower, tinged with color from her grandfather, who was a Moor. Her other grandfather was cousin to my own."

The old man closed his eyes. "Ah, Isabella—beauty beyond words! Her face, unflawed, resembling an angel, was unfit for ordinary men and challenged my unfailing courage just to look at her. Her supple limbs, her ample breasts! She moved as if she were performing a ballet, in graceful variations, and her body—it effused a scent, a sort of natural perfume, a floral fragrance that would cause a stir whenever she was in the company of men."

He stopped.

"Oh Isabella! —I was first to speak her name," he said. "We loved each other right away, and then my brother came to interfere. So I reminded him that I had made the first acquaintance and I asked that he should yield, but he was loath to quit her and ignored my claim. Instead, Fernando pressed his case without relent, beyond propriety! Because we were identical, he sought to make distinction favor him, so she might find a preference. He called me 'boorish and uneducated, crude and lacking any knowledge more than fighting bulls.'"

"Your brother said those things to her?" I asked.

"And worse!" he answered me. "I was not shy to fight, and so I parried in return. I said that facing danger in the ring provided me more insight than a man who flees could ever learn, by being soft and hiding inside shade and books.

"Ah, Isabella tried to bring civility, but what was she to do—caught in between two suitors who were same and opposite. She loved me as I was adventurous and rash, and easy in the company of danger from the world. And yet she loved Fernando too for being intellectual and cultured, stable and refined. *Ay-yi-yi-yi!*

"My father was interred beside my grandfather within Sevilla's 'Tomb of Matadors,' while Isabella went back to Madrid. Before she left, she promised me and promised him: *Within one year I will return to marry one of you.*"

He bowed his head, remembering, and looking up, he smiled. "Shall we have port?"

"*Divine!*" I answered with enthusiasm. Then the female servant poured a vintage port from Douro, this a precious nectar glimmering reddish-brown within the flickering light and shadows of the fireplace. I savored soft and lush complexity within its fruit grown oh so many years ago! And then I saw the label, covered all with dirt.

"The label on this wine says 1870!" I marveled as I took the bottle, brushing off the dust. "This port was made in 1870? *¿Verdaderamente?* You are drinking it with me?"

"Yes, only three are left," he said. "My oldest bottles from the cellar, stored at optimum conditions there." He raised his glass.

"A mi hermano! *A Fernando, el Ladrón!*"

I nodded, raising mine. "Yes, to Fernando, your beloved thief!"

"My first bullfight while as a matador was dueling with the murderer *Diablo*," Maestro said, "the bull that killed Gitano, causing cowardly Fernando to resign the ring. *Diablo* was a large and bitter dark brown bull with awful temperament. The gypsies said that he possessed a wicked spirit complement and he could not be killed, but I was unafraid. I only knew that he was dangerous and very smart. My father always taught that Castañeda de Castilla, we should rightly fear this bloodline in a bull.

"Within my hotel room that morning as I sat," *Señor* went on, "I had a conversation with the squire Gabriel, whose job it was to help me getting 'dressed to kill.' And as he helped to fix the *corbatín*, my narrow tie, he said a prayer for me and told me it was by no accident of fate that my first contest in the ring would be against *Diablo* on that day.

"Today is *Shabbat Shabbaton*," he said to me, "*Atonement Day*. You are the Priest before the people, and today you come to make atonement for inequities of humans crawling on the sand between the earth and sky. So you must spill compensatory blood to cleanse them from their sins. From all their sins, this sacrifice will make them clean before the Lord!"

"A *sacrifice, Señor?*" I sighed aloud while writing down his words. "I thought it was a bullfight you were in!"

"Of course!" *Señor* insisted. "At this sacred vernal gathering, commemorated by the trumpet blasts, I went out there before the crowd. But sacrificing bulls to save mankind is nothing new, my son. Religious holy men and cultures have been doing this throughout all time. The bullfight borrows from the ancient, sacred ceremonies of the past.

"Now whether I could call myself the archetypal matador, the great High Priest that day or not, I do not know. I *know* that when I killed *Diablo* on that afternoon—within that moment, I was certain that the bull within the ring was more than just a bull, and too the people watching were not merely entertained."

He paused and watched as Fátima refilled our glasses once again.

"The day I fought *Diablo*, then I understood there never really was a fleshly bull within the ring," he said while lowering his voice, as if to tell a secret hidden to the world. "The contest is with nature, not the bull. So there is only nature and the man, and then the nature *of* the man. The bull is just a symbol, just an emissary and an interface with nature and a link to something yet beyond this world. The matador, he must become at one with nature so to better understand the bull, so he can feel the bull, this to defeat the bull. But in the moment that a matador has ceased to *feel* the bull in that important way, then he will feel the horns of the unkind and unforgiving bull in yet another way."

"What happened with *Diablo*?" I inquired.

"He came out slow and cautious, studying me at first, a cunning creature," he began. "And then he tested me. He pawed the ground as if to start, and suddenly he stopped, or he would start and then abruptly change direction, hooking to one side or to the other, all the while premeditating murder. Then I noticed that *Diablo* tricked the banderilleros—then I saw that he was not so wounded by the darts as he allowed them to believe. His neck was strong with little injury, so he remained a mortal threat."

The maestro took the time to light a Bolivar cigar and puffed, the smoke emerging from corners of his mouth.

"But eventually I understood. I realized what he was doing, knew his very thoughts while he was thinking them," he said. "I knew what he was going to do before he even knew, and thus the dance. Oh, how the crowd was pleased. In all of their experience, this crowd had never watched a matador so skilled at mastering a bull, and mastering *Diablo* for their sins! For only then, they started calling me '*el Bailarín*.'"

He smiled, his mind returning to that time.

"Oh was *Diablo* angry, hating all the while the dance, and hating me! And he was panting wildly, grunting loudly, almost growling, if a bull could growl. And as he snorted in the dust and snorting out, it seemed he breathed hot flames and smoke from nose and mouth. With every pass, he led me, cheated just a little with his neck and tried to hook my abdomen. I knew his methods and was right beside him, matching passes, dancing close with him. If I had been remiss in any way, he would have gotten me, for I could feel his sweaty body close to mine, the power of his muscles and the beating of his heart. I knew I was the High Priest on that day and knew the people craved a sacrifice.

"And over time, *Diablo* finally began to show fatigue," he said, "though I exceeded time restraints. *El presidente* ordered trumpet blasts, the first ten minutes after we began, and two *avisos* meant as warnings to conclude the match. And yet the crowd and *Presidente* saw how strong and spirited *Diablo* was, beyond a natural bull. They recognized that this was something more than just a bullfight on that day! The contest lasted seven minutes more before I finally believed that I could safely thrust the *estocada*, or the stab with sword right through the heart of tiring *Diablo*, which I did accomplish with great style and art. His death was quick and clean, and thus the sins of all the people were atoned that day."

"And you defeated terrible *Diablo* in that match, your first?" I asked. "Did you believe that it was providence?"

"No question," he agreed. "I prayed and dedicated dead *Diablo's* body to the audience, to many who were from Hornos del Segura, the village where Gitano's family lived. *El Presidente* gave me both *Diablo's* ears, a fitting trophy, and his tail. I left the plaza on the shoulders of admirers. So from my very first performance, I became the favorite matador of all the people, loved by everyone.

Whenever or wherever I appeared, aficionados rushed into the plaza like a swarm of bees into a hive. "And there I was the priest, the expert at *suerte de matar*, which was 'the kill.' And so for seven glorious years the people celebrated me in all the places that I went—much like a movie star, with gifts, with privileges and women too—the finest found in Andalucía and all the world, but none so lovely and so captivating as the rare and pleasing Isabella from Zamora, near Madrid."

"Yes, Isabella!" I recalled. "And what became of her? Did she return back to Sevilla in one year to marry you or marry otherwise Fernando, as she promised both of you?"

"Ah yes," he said. "Within that year, Fernando and myself, we authored many letters to the lovely Isabella, the both of us, though separately of course, while she wrote letters back to us. And in one letter, she requested that I come to visit in Madrid, which I was all too pleased to do. It was the end of her requested year—in fact, the final month. I was most wonderfully surprised to get the invitation and I made great preparations, ordered gifts, accepted invitations to the palaces of grandees and their noble friends. I even made arrangements for an eminent appearance at plaza *Las Ventas*, where I would fight three bulls."

"So Isabella chose you over him?" I asked.

"She had invited me," he said, "to make determination whether she would marry me or wed Fernando in one month. And only after I was there did I discover that Fernando was invited too, at his insistence. He had come to visit also for one week, ahead of me. He left one day before I came. I thought it was not fair to me, but what else could I do? When friends of Isabella called me by the name 'Fernando,' I just smiled, and I corrected them."

"But you were angry? With Fernando or with Isabella?" I inquired.

"I was first-born, and also I was first to notice Isabella," he insisted, "so I should have been the first to court her, but Fernando, he ignored all rules, convention and propriety. Although aggressive passively, he pressed the fight. At every opportunity, he found a method to discredit and dishonor me. More than a teacher of philosophy, he taught his students pedagogics of the fight. Fernando was an expert at the rules and history, the moves and styles, so by the book, he had more knowledge in the art of bullfighting than anyone alive, though he had never faced a bull."

"*¡Ah qué traidor!*" I sighed, disgusted at Fernando. "What a treacherous man he was!"

"He was no traitor," Maestro said, correcting me. "There was no treachery. Fernando sought his own advantage, something that he thought was fair, and he expected just as much from me. I say that now, though I never would have said it then. While in Madrid, Fernando ushered Isabella to the opera and to ballet performances, to private concerts and to famous lecturers, to many cultured, fine events. Yet on his last day in Madrid, Fernando did the greatest harm. That was because he took her to a bullfight at the plaza *Las Ventas*.

"And while the fight was going on," *Señor* continued, "he explained to her the greater meaning of the actions in the ring. The first to fight a bull, he said, was Heracles, 'who in his seventh labor, with his empty hands subdued the Cretan Bull who was a plague upon the people there. And Theseus was next. He fought the same large bull, whose bloodline was again affliction to the people, and he slew him with a sword. And then he slew the Minotaur, who was half-bull, half-man, and who devoured many of the youth.

"It is one thing to kill domestic bulls for food or sacrifice, but quite another for a man to risk and to engage the fleshly bull in contest to the death. To do it on behalf of ordinary people and to *conquer* it, to make atonement for their sins,' he told the crowd at *Las Ventas*, 'that hero is the matador!'

"'Yet only the enlightened matador,'" he said, "'can recognize the spiritual significance of symbols in the match. The bull epitomizes nature, the unbridled sin within the man, beginning first with wrath, then lust, then pride and envy, and the contest is a struggle, is a fight against and victory over them. The plaza is the public stage, or temple grounds, where people are inspired to take up this spiritual battle in their private lives.

"'The matador who lacks enlightenment,' he said, 'this man becomes a victim of the sin that he was born to fight against. This man is vain and hateful, carnal, proud and jealous. My own brother called Antonio is such a matador, who struggles in the dark, as I have heard and seen. He hates his flesh, and willing captives of his empty conquests in the night would fill the seats of this arena here and standing room besides.

"And yet, he is too proud to realize he is a victim of the very bulls he fights. I love my brother, though I pity him. Before the people he is priest and champion, but in the fight against his imperfection, in the struggle for enlightenment, he failed the battle on that day he faced *Diablo* and he lost his soul."

The old man sipped the last from *porto* glass and turned it upside down while looking in.

"Perhaps a second bottle then?"

"Why not?" I answered, swallowing the last from my own glass. "Your brother said those things to poison Isabella's heart?"

"No, not at all," he disagreed. "Fernando said those things because he thought those things were true, and he was right to some degree. When I was young, I did not understand the things I understand today. And Isabella was not turned *from* me. His words instead stirred curiosity and then desire, as I later learned. But what he said turned her *toward* him, toward intellect and culture, and security. Upon the *lendeman*, Fernando left, and then I came."

The maestro called to Fátima and asked her for a second bottle of the port. He poured for us and then symbolically for her, because she would not drink.

"My first day in Madrid," he said, "I was a special feature at the plaza *Las Ventas*, and where I fought against three bulls. And oh, the crowds, they loved me, shouting, *"Manolete! Manolete! Manolete!"* and pronouncing me the newest champion of Spain. It was a glorious day."

"I planned to take her to a special dinner in my honor at the palace of the Duke Luis Carrero-Blanco," Señor said, "but Isabella had decided that we would not go. Instead, she made a reservation at *Ingles Hotel*, and said that we should go there right away. And once inside the room, she wanted to make love, and I obliged—on thirty-three occasions on that day."

"On *thirty-three* occasions!" I exclaimed. "But that's impossible!"

"Extraordinary? Yes," he said. "Incredible, I *know*, but not impossible. And on the second day, I thought to take her to a movie set, where an American, a Hollywood producer came to make a film about my life. But once again, she wanted to remain within the room to practice more at making love. I was fatigued of course, and perhaps a little sore, so only twenty-one occasions on that second day. And on the third, her appetite was growing still, and on the fourth and fifth as well. So when the week that I was in Madrid was

over, all we had accomplished was to make love and to eat, to eat
and then make love, with only periods of sleep between."

"Then Isabella chose to marry you?" I asked.

"You did not let me finish," he insisted. "It was on the night
before the day I would return back home, and thinking of the week
I had with her, I thought for certain she had chosen me. Fernando
never was a virile man. It would have been impossible for him to
match my fleshly feats in bed, and Isabella was a sensual and
passionate young bull, and with an appetite that grew with each
lascivious course it ate. But she surprised me on that day."

"How so?" I asked.

"*She chose my brother*," he replied. "She told me that she loved
me, but she said that I was not the type of man that she or any other
healthy-minded woman wanted for a husband. Disappointed and
confused, I asked her why. I felt a mortal wound. A horn impaled
my heart to hear those words!"

"You are a matador, Antonio—so handsome, virile,
overconfident. You have enjoyed your women by the hundreds,
maybe more," she said, "so who am I to count among so many stars?
Consider what we shared a gift, for you received the pleasures of
my body, and without condition or expense to you. You had your
conquest over me and you devoured me until exhausting all your
want."

"'But I'm in love with you!' I passionately declared," he said to
her. "The stars are countless in the skies, and yet there only is one
sun. And when that sun arrives, the shining stars will fade and
disappear. The time we shared is but a minute in the early
afternoon. We have a glorious day ahead of us!"

"Yes," sadly Isabella sighed, "although eventually the day will
pass and then the sun will set, just as it always does, and you,
Antonio, then you'll go back to counting stars, perhaps within
another city at a future time, the nameless, faceless women you will
have. For after conquest with the bull is through will follow
conquest of the women too. It is your nature. You cannot control
yourself."

"That is not true!" he argued. "Not with me and never more! I
stand beneath your sun from now until I die!"

"Oh, carnal men like you," she said, "mistake the sun for the
inconstant moon, which shines so brightly for a time, perhaps a
night or two, and then it disappears. You stand in moonlight and

in starlight, thinking all the while you stand beneath the sun. *¡Ay, Dios mío!* You must be yourself, Antonio. I thoroughly enjoyed our seven glorious days and nights while lying under you, while being unpredictable, the inconsistent moon, or as a twinkling star.

"I know that men like you are meant to pleasure carnal women, make them feel the greatest ecstasy. You did not disappoint. So like a wild, unbridled bull you were! I loved the sheer excitement and the passion that you brought for me. But men like you are never meant for marrying, so I will marry your twin brother, inexperienced Fernando, when I come again to southern Spain. He is the better choice."

"I fell in love with Isabella long before that day," the old man quietly explained. "I did not substitute the sun for moon, as I had never known the cast and character of love until that very moment when I lost the first and final woman I would ever love," he said. "I stood when she arose because I had to know."

"And did you do this same thing with my brother also, with Fernando, when he came to visit you?" I asked.

"I never for one time considered it," she said. "*For men you think that you might wed, you save yourself for marriage bed,* 'according to my prudent aunt.' Think what you want of it."

Señor returned to me and to the present time.

"*¡Cornada!* I remember it so clearly on that morning and the way she looked at me just then as she declared— 'Think what you want of it.' Ah, never had I had such longing sadness in my heart before! It was the first time in my life I knew that I felt love. An unmistakable and poignant incident, still burning in my memory. And such a moment can reshape the human heart. Do you remember it, Morisco, that first moment in your life?"

Surprised by such a private question, I could not remember such a time initially. I stuttered as I answered, summoning regret.

"Ah yes, I do, *Señor.*"

"Then you have truly lived!" he said before he bowed his head and sighed. "So Isabella came back to Sevilla that next month and married with my brother. I did not attend the wedding, nor would I congratulate the happy couple. I was angry and resentful since I felt that I was wronged. And that is when I then began to call my brother *el Ladrón*—the thief who stole my love and happiness. But I was angry also with revengeful Isabella, who by spurning me avenged the many women who had loved me and who longed for me to no avail, to only see me move so quickly to the next. In irony I mused that Isabella must have known what she had done to me, and how she crushed my heart.

"For three full years I did not count another star, not one!" he said. "For three whole years I wandered in the dark beneath a starless, moonless sky! Whenever I allowed myself to think of her, the sun was there for just that time, and then there was the mocking thought that my own brother stole the woman who I loved, had taken her, exploiting carnal treasures meant for me! It was a time of bitter darkness when I hated him for blackening my sky. Oh how I hated him, Fernando, my own brother, who had stole the sun. How I despised Fernando for that theft!"

He wiped a tear that trailed along his wrinkled cheek.

"That hate, I let it transform me. It changed my aspect and it made me cynical. While in the ring, I ceased to dance with bulls, no longer made concessions to the gallery. Instead, I would imagine, just before the *estocada*, or the final thrust—I wished my brother was the bull and I could drive my sword into his heart.

"My prudent squire, Gabriel," Señor recalled, "who noted my behavior being dark, he warned me as he dressed me once before a match. He said to me, 'Fernando is your brother, flesh and blood, Antonio, and while you say he has offended you, if you yourself do not forgive, then sin is crouching at your door; and its desire is to master you, but you must master it instead. Consider Cain, a twin like you,' he said, 'who learned that one who kills his brother kills himself.'"

"I did not listen," Maestro then explained, "and I continued to resent Fernando and to dwell upon the injury that I believed he caused to me. So monstrous grew my hate that it distorted my own face and made me cruel and arrogant while fighting bulls. So after time, I was not loved as much by all the people of Sevilla, those who recognized in Andalucía my change of character, yet I remained still popular throughout the rest of Spain and Mexico and South America."

"And all this for a woman?" I inquired. "Is any woman so incredible to make a man despise his brother, hating his own flesh?"

"To my regret, 'yes,'" he admitted. "Isabella truly was that wonderful."

"Fernando then," I asked, "he hated you as well?"

"He did," Antonio affirmed. "I saw him at my mother's funeral, that being four years after he had married Isabella. We were rivals, so we saw each other through necessity. There I discovered then that he resented me as much as I resented him, and for an equal cause: for Isabella's love."

"He married Isabella, *Sí*? Fernando got the girl!" I said, perplexed. "What reason would he have to hate Antonio?"

"He won the hand of Isabella, yes, but not her heart," *Señor* explained, "for she was miserable with him, a circumstance that made him very much aggrieved. That much was obvious at the funeral, and yet Fernando had become a tyrant to the world to live a lie. He was exceedingly intelligent, but he was spiteful and contemptuous of those who he believed were ignorant in comparison, and that included everyone. Like me, he was estranged from destiny to be a matador."

"And did you speak to one another at your mother's funeral?" I asked.

"It was our showdown, a *corrida de hermanos*, played before the family, before the world who watched," he said. "Then I began by telling him, 'You wronged me first, Fernando. In the contest for the prize of Isabella's hand, you treated me without familial respect. Instead of courting her by telling her the finest attributes in you, you sought to win her by creating and promoting the defect in me, and you succeeded by employing trickery and lying to discredit me. You are dishonorable, my brother. By the heavens, spoken by a prudent king, *the treasures of the wicked profit none!* So you will have to pay some retribution for your treachery!'"

"He looked upon the sword within my hand," Señor detailed, remembering. "'What? Will you kill me now, Antonio?' Fernando asked. 'And will you murder your own brother here before your family and before the world? And why? Because you lost the contest for our Isabella's heart?

"'You truly are a beast, Antonio, just like the bulls you fight! Your very actions show that I am honest and more honorable. I saved her from your savagery. You are a base and simple-minded brute with bloody hands who never did deserve her heart. You are a cursed bullfighter and so your destiny will be to die ignobly in the ring one day, just like the many soulless bulls that you have slaughtered there.'"

"But I would rather die a bloody death within the ring," Antonio then answered, "than to live a discontented life, while hiding in between the pages of your dusty books! You ran away, Fernando, coward that you are! You saw Gitano killed, and turning white with fear, you abandoned destiny, and after that you built a wall of books around yourself to hide that fear, both from the world and from yourself. Yet you have never lived a single day of glory of the life you craved. You saw his blood and turned away. But you have never faced your fear, have never faced yourself. You never faced a bull, Fernando, physical or spiritual, *except for in a book!*

"Your life is counterfeit, so I would rather suffer pain and violence, having lived and in control of my own life, as I face death. And I would welcome death than rather to exist in fear, in hiding and a victim of your over-cautious thinking. You are smarter than I am, Fernando—I admit—but I am wise before you are. I learned while young there is a time to stop considering and rather get things done. For live or die—live *till* you die! The men who live, they act! And men who think—they often fashion coffins for themselves, composed of worry and regret. You won the hand of Isabella, yes, but only time will tell before she realizes she is married to a man who is afraid to live. You have not begun to be alive!"

"In wisdom, Isabella favored me," Fernando countered, "this because she knows your decadence and sees the mindless creature that you are, a stud-bull in the stables and a victim of disgusting fleshly, carnal inclinations. You are but an animal who does not understand the spiritual. Within a beast, your qualities are admirable and worthy of *indulto*. In a man, however, they are undesirable, detestable to women such as Isabella. You have not begun to think."

"My life within the ring has taught me that a man can overcome his nature," said Antonio, "yes even you, Fernando. But to overcome, you then must stop in flight, stop hiding, turn and face your destiny. Why don't you close your books for once and come into the living, breathing, *bleeding* world that is the source of knowledge and of books. Fernando, brother, look into your heart and rediscover who you are!"

"On hearing me so passionate," the old man said, "Fernando bowed his head and he began to think, which was not good I thought—his thinking there. But then he whispered, asking me to meet him later in a private place, away from all the ears and tongues who heard our argument."

"So I agreed to meet him for this rendezvous," the maestro said. "We met within our family home, within the parlor where, as boys, we spent much time together with our father, listening to his stories all about the bullfights and the celebrated matadors. Within this very room where we are sitting talking now! In this same room, we dreamed of being best in all the world, twin matadors, the pride of Andalucía, and dearest friends besides."

The elderly Antonio reflected for a moment, silently remembering.

"I do not know how soon Fernando thought of it, but I considered it at once," he said. "Perhaps he was inviting me away to such a private place in order to impair or murder me! I knew I would not come there unprepared, which meant unarmed, and so I brought my sword. When I arrived, I saw the light was on, and carefully, I entered on my toes and eased along, my sword prepared to strike. And when I got inside the room, I looked across to see Fernando, sitting in an armchair, pointing a revolver right at me, directly at my heart. I stopped at once."

"So you invited me to shoot me dead?" Antonio inquired. "Fernando, what we have... is failure to communicate!"

Fernando only laughed and then he said, "Your mind is always at the cinema, Antonio! You heard that line while watching movies from America? But no?" He raised the gun and pointed toward the ceiling. 'No. This pistol?" he announced, "I brought it for defense.'"

"From what?" Antonio requested of his counterpoint.

"From you," Fernando answered, motioning toward the weapon in his brother's hand. "What was your plan for me to think to bring a sword?"

Antonio returned the sword to sheath and placed it on the table, then he raised his arms. "Protection on my part," he said. "If you have plans to shoot me, do it now. I have no fear. You took from me the single thing I wanted in the world, my Isabella, so I have no want to live. Please shoot me now if that is what you planned."

Fernando placed the gun, unloaded, on the tabletop. He shrugged and wagged his head.

"Your words are droll, irrational, Antonio, since as a favor, I was going to beg of you to stab me on tonight, right through the heart."

"But why?" Antonio demanded then. "You won and now have Isabella! You have education and respect from all the world. And still you are unsatisfied? Please tell me why?"

"When you have never *lived*," Fernando sad admitted, "does it really matter? I was born, like you, to be a matador, and here I am—astronomer instead of astronaut. I pondered on the points we argued earlier, and you were right. Perhaps I *never have begun to be alive*. I fled from destiny, and that is why I wish to offer a proposal as a proof, Antonio," he said.

"You offer a proposal to do what?" his brother asked.

"I know that you believe I am a coward, always hiding in the books, too careful, so dishonorable and afraid to live?" Fernando summarized. "So you believe all this, while I believe that you are base, uncivilized and ignorant to the real significance of life and to the purpose and the duty of the matador. Is this the truth?"

"Well, yes," Antonio affirmed.

"Then I propose this offer on today," Fernando said. "We are two mirror-image twins, so I propose that for one day, for one day only—we will trade our places, both of us. Then you will go into the university to teach in place of me—and I will journey to the plaza so that I can fight a bull in place of you. Thus in one day our unresolved debate will end and we will see who has the better argument."

Antonio, he was amused at the absurdity of what Fernando offered him. "You cannot fight a bull!" he laughed.

"You cannot teach!" Fernando then rebutted in return. "So let us see which argument prevails, and then perhaps the both of us will learn from this experience to stop this judging one another and to understand our lives from differing perspectives. And perhaps two brothers who have been estranged for many years will learn to love each other once again."

"I hesitated as I wondered if it was a trick," Antonio recalled, "though when I realized that he was serious, I finally agreed. He had insisted on this switching places at the soonest opportunity, and so it happened that it was the week before *Feria de Abril Sevilla*, or the Sevillano Springtime Fair, which made it perfect then. With bullfights fought on weekdays during all the festival, we could on one day simply trade our places. I would go into the university one afternoon to face the intellect of youth and of established education. He would go into the plaza then to face an angry bull."

The stunning Fátima returned and cleared the plates and poured more wine for us. Then smiling maestro paused, reflecting, and continued when we were alone again.

"Ah well, the week flew by, and hour to a minute. As I thought about our deal, I realized Fernando had a clear advantage over me, since after all, my brother was a picador, a banderillero and a Novillero earlier in life. He had experience to be a matador, but me—I did not know one paragraph of teaching, learning or philosophy. And so, within that week I realized my brother was correct, that I was purely physical, the same as all the bulls I fought. My wood was wet and green, and yet the fire only then began to burn. I was a very different person at that time.

"The day was on a Friday," he recalled, "a tepid Friday afternoon. The orange and olive trees were blossoming again and in the grassy pastures, springtime poppies and the purple flowers were in bloom. The little yellow flowers were all over too. Fernando met me here before our family home that morning, so that we could trade our clothes and cars. I noticed right away that he was nervous too. His hands were shaking, but upon his face, I saw determination—jaw held tight with purpose in his eyes. I knew he conquered all his fear within and he was ready to confront the bull. Fernando was prepared to live that day."

"My hands were shaking too," Señor admitted. "I had no idea of what to do or say when finally I was to stand before his classes with the aim to teach them anything. I read two books that week, two college books, whose author was Fernando, since I thought that reading them would make me more prepared, but learning little only proved to me how much I did not know. Fernando, on that morning, hugged me for the first in ten years' time. We wished success for one another and wept as we departed on that day."

The hand-rolled, redolent cigar burned slowly in the ashtray, cherry glowing brightly red. Señor blew out a cloud of smoke and spoke.

"I traveled to the school and parked the auto of my brother in his space," he said. "Fernando left for me instructions, showing where to go and what to do and where the classroom was. To me, my brother proved to be extraordinary on that day, when seeing how he was so loved and well respected at the university. Associate professors, staff and students were all smiles and pleased to see me there. I followed carefully what he had said to do, and all went well until I stood before the class, embarrassed, ignorant and dumb."

"Today," Antonio announced at last before the class, "instead of me instructing you, I want to hear from you what you have learned, and what I've taught to you. Now who would like to start?"

The students seemed confused at first, until one happy, smiling beautiful young woman rose to speak.

"The bullfight," she declared, "it represents the love affair between a woman and a man, an intricate erotic dance involving danger and deception, blood and passion, flesh and spirit, heart and mind. It is a serious and solemn business with momentous consequences, yet the outcome favors neither matador or bull.

"The man is matador, and thus the woman, like the bull, becomes the object of this match. The man's desire is to train, wear down and to subdue the woman, while the woman will assert her independence, cunning, strength and power over him. The man who feels and understands the woman—he will have success, and both will win. And yet the woman lacking loyalty will also lose, since she will never find his heart."

Antonio, who listened as "Fernando," stood there pleasantly surprised by such profound and thoughtful allegory from the pretty girl.

"I taught you this?" he asked.

"You lectured on this matter for three days. It was my favorite," she said. "You seemed so passionate about this dance between a man and woman through a span of life. I never will forget the way I felt to hear your words and know your heart. And only after that, I understood the allegory of the bullfight... and of love."

"Well, thank you, Señorita," young Antonio replied and seemed to blush. "Will someone else reveal what you have learned from me?"

A thin young man who wore thick glasses stood and spoke, and with an accent beckoning Madrid.

"The matador resembles most the true believer, living in a vast society of unbelievers, where the true believer loves his God, his neighbor and himself. The proper matador will understand his job and does it from the inside out."

"How from the inside out?" Antonio inquired.

"Of course, I'm quoting now a classic theologian whose ideas you shared with us," the young man said. "In every action that the matador performs, it signifies a smaller part within a larger series of a greater ritual. So method counts, skill counts, as well as dedication to the purpose, just as virtue matters. Once the fear of death is overcome, then life in full can be appreciated in its highest form. In contrast, the dishonest matador, like nominal believers, is only 'skillful technically.' He 'takes no pleasure in the *art* of fighting bulls, deriving no emotion, elevation or elation from his work.'"

"And so I spent the balance of my time," Señor recalled, "in learning what my brother taught his class, and only then I realized my twin already was a matador, though in a separate way of seeing things. These students, they were teaching me, and after listening to Fernando's students on that day, then finally I understood. I needed to become a man of learning too, just as he was."

Again, he sipped the wine.

"Then in the final class," the maestro said, "one student noticed I was standing to the left side of the chalkboard, writing with my right hand, while my brother always stood along the right and wrote then with his left. She noticed it in passing, but it fueled a sudden fear in me."

"You see, Morisco" Maestro said, "the *cuadrilla*—my own team of picadors and banderilleros at the plaza—toreadors, they would prepare, would wound the bull and place the darts in advantageous places, thinking that Fernando was Antonio. And they would not allow the bull to hook or favor right, a strategy that made the bull less dangerous to me because I was right-handed, while Fernando used his left! At school, it was a mere discerning insight by an undergraduate, but in the bullring, it meant life or death. *¡Mi hermano mismo!* I had to hurry to the plaza to avert a tragedy!"

"When I arrived and rushed into *La Maestranza*," Antonio recalled, "Fernando, in my place, was just beginning his first fight. The bull was rather small, a *Vistahermosa* there with thin and pointed horns—*astifino*, though a creature full of spirit. As I watched Fernando in the early passes he completed, oh his execution was elaborate, unflawed, beginning with a clean *verónica* before *a rebolera*! Later, when the picadors and the banderilleros left the scene, then he was calm and graceful as he worked the animal to show frustration and fatigue. *¡Pase de la firma! ¡Afarolado!* Still I see it my mind until this day! He even managed to perform a *manoletina*! It was beautiful to watch!

"It was a well-fought match," he said, "his very first! The crowd was pleased, and they kept calling out my name: ¡el Bailarín! ¡el Bailarín! ¡ole! I found it strange to hear my name while someone else was in the ring. Yet eventually, there came 'a time to kill.' I worried for Fernando as he paused before he lunged into *volapié*. This act presents the greatest danger for a matador. It is the moment of unvarnished truth.

I held my breath as he performed the *estocata*, and he did so with such fluid motion and decisiveness and with such grace that all the audience sighed loud in awe of him. The way the bull succumbed, the way it tumbled to the sand, was poetry beheld. Fernando had impressed me for a second time that day, a day forever in my memory."

The *maestro* raised his wineglass to the sky. "*Brindis por el valiente Fernando y ese glorioso día!*" he proclaimed.

I raised my glass to toast the memory. "To brave Fernando and that glorious day!"

"When I went down to speak with him," the maestro said, "when after celebration ceased and he was then awarded trophies by *el presidente*, then I told him I was very proud to have a brother who had fought so well. I also told him to enjoy and safeguard his good fortune, telling him we should exchange our clothes again so I should fight the final bull. I warned him that this bull was a *Miura*, smart and dangerous. *Muerte* he was called, because he was a bull who hated humankind."

"*Muerte*? Death?" I mused. "Yet why chose such a fear-inspiring name for just a bull?"

"He was a dreadful, bull," Señor assured. "*Muerte* was a coal-black animal with eyes of red and black. He had big muscles in the haunches and the thickest neck I ever saw. He was a true *Catedral*, meaning he was very large, with forward-facing horns. There also was an odd and inauspicious omen in this bull: his body had no hair! A hairless, black-skinned bull, and worse, his bloodline was not favorable to Castañeda de Castilla. Worse, it was our nemesis.

"The bloodline knows the vine from which it springs, and so the bloodline of *Diablo*, who I routed first in my career, was seeking retribution for his slaughter on the sand. The other matadors and I, we first took notice of this bull when he was three years old, when he could not be stirred to anger or emotion like the other bulls. His reddish eyes, infernal gateways to his bitter hate for man—he held them low. We knew that he was always watching us with murder on his mind. As matadors, we did not fear, but none of us were eager to engage this bull."

"My proud and stubborn brother would not have it so," the maestro said. "Fernando on that day insisted he would fight the final bull. The taste of blood had made him drunk, and so his courage swelled beyond his common sense."

"You have already proved yourself," Antonio advised, "but you cannot contest *Muerte* and remain alive. Be pleased that you have conquered fear! Enjoy the glory you have earned, Fernando. I admire you and love you from my heart. Now *I* will fight *Muerte* and you must assume your proper disposition in the stands."

"Here we have tempted Fate and traded places for one day," Fernando countered then, "although this day is barely underway! The sun is high. For one day only I will be Antonio, for all the good or woe the day might bring, for all that I must learn, and only after it is over will I be restored to my own life and you to yours. Today the die is cast, our fates forever intertwined."

"But I insist, Fernando," spoke Antonio with urgency. "This is no more a contest judging who is right or wrong, and this is not an intellectual experiment. Three proven matadors are here today, who understand the bloodline of this bull. Not one of them would like to face *Muerte*, given choice. The *sorteo*, the 'lot' for him, was cast and Fate appointed him to me and not to you. We must exchange our clothes again so I can fight this bull!"

Fernando turned. He walked away and looked to where the *cuadrilla*, or the team, was readying the bull for entrance of the picadors. He looked back toward Antonio.

"*Muerte* merely is a bull," he said. "A bull I must defeat!"

"Not true," Antonio insisted. "I have learned from what you taught your students in the class. *Muerte* is much more than just a bull. *Muerte* is a manifestation coming from the universe, a dire reminder that the lives and the ambitions of mere men are vanity. You have already killed a bull. You conquered fear within and have become the man you wished to be, so there is nothing else to prove."

"You do not understand," Fernando then retorted, "that this moment is my trial, a rendezvous with destiny that I avoided my entire life. I have not told you this, but not one week ago, a gypsy woman came to me and she predicted that this day and moment would arrive. She said you would be here. She knew we would be standing here—right at this very spot! And finally, she said that I was meant to fight *Muerte* on this day, and live!"

"What you are saying now, Fernando, is impossible!" Antonio declared. "The name of this *Miura* never was *Muerte*. That is only what the matadors are calling him. His name is from the ranch where he was born and called *Vitatribuo*, so this gypsy could have never known one week ago you would be here today and that the matadors had named this bull *Muerte* not two days ago! Besides, she could not know we would be here, and this would be our circumstance! One week ago today we made this deal!"

Antonio, he tried to hold his brother back before Fernando stepped out from the *burladero*, but his brother snatched himself away.

"¿*Vitatribuo*? ¡*Alabado sea dios!*" said Fernando then. "This older woman of Triana told me I must fight this bull. This very bull! She told me that this bull would give me life!"

Antonio tried to stop his counterpart, intoxicated by the passion of the fight, from going out onto the plaza sand, but yet the *alguacilillo*, the official on the horse, he would not let him in the ring. And so Fernando stood out there still clad in *trajes de luces* of Antonio. He watched the picadors, who tried to stir *Muerte* to attack the padded horses under them.

"Through signals with his hands, Antonio directed both the picadors to violently abuse *Muerte*, punish with severity the muscular *murillo* of the bull in order to provide Fernando with a better chance. The clever animal was wary, so he kept his distance to avoid the hand of Fate. So by the time the trumpets blasted to begin the second third, *Muerte* bled, but not so much as apprehensive, guilt-possessed Antonio had wanted him to bleed. *Muerte* still was very strong.

And next the banderilleros came with pointed darts, the decorated wooden sticks, but then Fernando called them off, insisting he would place the *banderillas* by himself. He was, according to my memory, the finest banderillero at the school when we were training in Carmona to be matadors.

"So running toward *Muerte*, spirit warrior Fernando got the bull to charge him, waiting to the last before he swerved and spun and feinted one direction, while he bolted in another way. And as the bull went by, he drove the pointed arrow deep into the muscle of the neck. *Muerte*'s head then dropped a little. On the second pass, another stick, placed on the other side. Aficionados cheered his brave audacious style!

"Fernando proved himself a virtuoso on that day," Antonio admitted with a smile. "The crowd became excited, eager to enjoy this match, and they applauded many times his artistry. And finally enraged, *Muerte* tossed his body and he snorted while retreating, backing up against the *barrera*, still outside the chalk-drawn circle there. The trumpet sounded, and it was at last the man against the bull.

"Fernando came out first," Antonio remembered, seeing in his mind the spectacle, "while holding the *muleta* and *estoque* in his left hand, the *montera* in his right. He bowed before *el presidente*, asking for consent to slay *Muerte* on that afternoon.

"Before the crowd, he proudly dedicated the *Miura* to his brother called Fernando, who was 'watching from the stands.' And as the crowd applauded, there I stood embarrassed, in my brother's place. Such irony—by dedicating this impressive bull to me, Fernando was unwittingly bequeathing ominous *Muerte* to himself. He tossed his hat, his *montera*, to me. I caught it, looking in his eyes, neither brother realizing that the moment would forever change our lives."

Señor continued, eyes glazed over as the years-old footage played upon the film-encrusted pupils of his eyes.

"My brother in his first approach was bold and daring," he recalled. "Fernando dropped down to his knees while holding el *muleta*, or the cape, in front of him, and tempting hot *Muerte* to the fight. The bull stepped forward, studying the situation and position of the banderilleros. Then he charged with shocking speed directly toward my brother, who was fearless and remaining motionless until he felt *Muerte*'s breath.

"Fernando next, with unbelievable agility, he spun and quickly stepped aside while waving wide the scarlet cloth and disappearing to another place. His movement had deceived our eyes, as I was certain that I saw the blur of shadowy *Muerte*, though incorporeal, which seemed to pass directly through Fernando's form. The crowd was shocked at first. They thought *Muerte* surely killed the matador, but he was standing there beside the bull—triumphant and unscathed. My ears can hear it now, as the applause and cheers were deafening!"

Astonished by the episode, I could not write it down, though I was pleased the tape was still recording. I was mesmerized.

"I must admit I was surprised by how dexterously my brother fought this bull," *Señor* explained, the images still playing in my mind. "Especially since he had never faced an actual bull before that day. And next, he led *Muerte* in a flight of passes that exposed his flaws and weaknesses. It was amazing watching this frustrated bull, so powerless within the order of the universe. *Muerte* knew his place and brave Fernando knew his proper place."

"The fight went on ten minutes time," Antonio continued. "*Muletazo, pase de rodillas, gaonera, parar, aragonesa.* If a matador could fight one bullfight in his life, I think that he would want to give the best performance possible, and that is what I watched, the perfect bullfight in a *pasadoble* I had never seen in all my life, and not before or since that day. I still recall the envy that I felt. My brother, who had been a coward all his life and who had never fought a bull, to see him first engage to dominate so formidable a bull in such a way I could have never dreamt to do. He fought a faultless fight against the smartest, strongest most ferocious bull that all the world had ever seen, his dominance extraordinary on that day.

"And after then, the second bugle blast. The moment came when he should kill this bull. Fernando showed enormous patience while preparing *denouement*. The bull was tired, panting there. *Muerte* was subdued within the time my brother went to switch the wooden imitation for a sword of steel. His task was next to bring *Muerte's* feet together so to open up his shoulder blades, thus setting up an opportunity to implement the mortal stroke. He did this with a final series of *muleta* passes that positioned the fatigued *Muerte* at the center of the ring."

The maestro's voice took on a hallowed tone.

"The moment of authentic truth—which is the instant that the matador will take his greatest chance. You see, to thrust and pierce the heart of any bull, the matador assumes the utmost risk by going past the horns. It is the difference between magnificence and ignominy, a fine distinction, and Fernando did not disappoint. His *estocada*, or the mortal stroke was, as they say, pure poetry in motion, and the audience stood silently, enraptured as *Muerte* stopped in place and sank down to his knees, and then the blood began to flow. He keeled to earth while favoring one side, his body quivering, relinquishing four years of life.

"But then we saw Fernando," Maestro said. "Yes, he had killed the bull, but on the fabric of his *trajes de luces* was a growing crimson stain. He raised his arms and staggered several paces— then he fell onto the sand. And all at once, the cheering stadium was silent as we watched him try to rise, to only fall again. And after that, we knew that it was *cornada*, that somehow Fernando had been gored!"

He wiped away the tears from moistened eyes.

"I screamed his proper name aloud," *Señor* remembered, "but my voice was drowned out by the roar of people in the plaza calling my own name. Fernando had been gored, and mortally perhaps, but all of Spain was thinking it was me. The women and the girls were crying, and the men were pounding on their chests as even *Presidente* sadly sank into his seat. A legendary matador had suffered a defeat, and at that moment he lay writhing, struggling, even dying there beside *Muerte* on the plaza sand. They all believed that it was me out there! They were amazed and they were calling it the greatest bullfight of all time, in all of history! And they were calling me the greatest matador who ever lived!

"And that was the beginning of my dire predicament," *Señor* admitted with a shrug. "In panic, without thinking, I ran toward the barrier, and leaping over it onto the sand, I sprinted toward Fernando lying there. And when at last I reached him, he was on his back, and choking on an overwelling mouth of blood. The doctor was already there to sit him up, to help him spit the blood. And right away, I saw the wound below his ribs was gushing blood in imitation of his beating heart. I saw this sort of injury before. The horn had gone into his lung and possibly into the area around his heart. It was not good."

The maestro's sympathetic hand caressed the place on his own chest where poor Fernando felt the wound.

"I stood in horror and in shock," he said. "That moment kept on playing in my head, once over, then again! When earlier I saw it from the stands, I hoped with all my heart my eyes deceived, but it was unmistakable: within the instant that Fernando lunged to plunge the sword into the heart of diabolical *Muerte*, then the angry bull was quick to yank its neck off to one side, and upward to the right at once. His horn was piercing deep into Fernando's lower chest and slipping out with yet another motion from the bull, and thus the *estocada* of *Muerte*, tragically, was even more poetic than the *estocada* of Fernando. As I looked across the plaza at the bull, he snorted loud a final time while looking at my brother, as if finding satisfaction that he had avenged his death."

Another tear and then another sip of port the maestro swallowed without savoring.

"It was not long before the priest was there," *Señor* recalled. "And by that time, my team had brought out blankets and a *camilla*... how do they call it in America? A stretcher? Yes, but they were too afraid to move him as the blood was gushing through the bandages. Expression grave, the cleric bowed his head and spoke a silent prayer."

"Two minutes, maybe five," the priest announced. "It's all the time that he has left, so you must speak the final words to him that you will ever speak while in this world. When you are done, I will return to then administer *viaticum* and to perform the final rites. You are Fernando, brother of Antonio, his twin? If not already done, then you must make your peace with him before he dies."

"So there I was," Señor acknowledged, "with my dying brother, at the center of the plaza, with an audience of thousands looking on, and with the world too looking on, and even God was looking as Fernando raised a hand to summon me. The doctors who attended to Fernando yielded space to let us speak in private as he died.

"Antonio!" Fernando begged. "Forgive me, please! A sacrament of penance I must speak before I die!"

Antonio, he bowed his head, remembering a lifetime with his brother, dying there. "A penance is not necessary from you now," he strained to utter. "Isabella willingly chose you. You won her heart because you are a worthy man, and brave. I saw an extraordinary matador today! There is no error to forgive."

"There is!" Fernando groaned while struggling to sit upright. "You do not understand! You cannot see what is before you now? Now I am truly *el Ladrón*. I do not mean to, but today I steal your death and give to you my life! The gypsy did not lie. Can you not see? I am not dying in the plaza here today! Today *you* die, Antonio!"

"I slowly raised my eyes," the old man said, "and when I saw my team and the officials and *el presidente* and the saddened, murmuring crowd of spectators, I realized at last what he was telling me. We told *no one* we traded places, therefore everyone believed that it was me, Antonio Castañeda de Castilla, everyone believed that I was dying in the ring that day! To my astonishment, I knelt beside him, disinclined to witness my own **death!**"

The maestro leaned toward me, his voice conveying secrecy.

"But we must tell the world **what we have done!**" Antonio strained to whisper in a panic to Fernando lying there. "I cannot die today! My life cannot be forfeit—there are things I want to do!"

"Forgive me please, Antonio," Fernando said. "You must forgive, but you can never tell what we have done—to anyone, since it would be a fraud for which you would be utterly disgraced, to have allowed your brother, who had never fought a bull before this day, to have him face *Muerte* in your place.

"Say nothing, and I die in glory. Tell what we have done, and you will live in shame. Just look around and see how much Sevilla loves Antonio and see how all of Spain admires him! So die in peace. Your name will live in glory from this moment on."

Antonio, he looked again to feel the spirit of the crowd and did not know what he should do. It all had happened very fast. He was not ready to relinquish his successful life, but Fate had left no choice. And then, Fernando, dying there, he had no choice.

Fernando forced himself to smile, his blood-soaked lips becoming black.

"Is it so bad?" he asked, "since you will finally have Isabella, after all. So in the sequel, you have won."

Antonio bowed his head, the old man said, while thinking for the first of what his life would be to trade his very soul with someone else. Fernando lived a life of wealth and ease and intellectual celebrity, and yet Antonio would rather to have had his own.

"But I have won as well!" Fernando said. "I die for you, and yet I am not sad today. And what a day! It has bestowed the greatest glory in a plaza ever seen in Spain! How fortunate I am to die upon the finest day I ever lived! So you were right, Antonio. Yes, all along, my life was wrong and yours was right!"

"But you have lost your life, Fernando!" sad Antonio said, "so how could I be right?"

"Because our lives are not so much a matter made of watching action from the stands," Fernando said, "or reading of the life, adventure and the danger we desire in our books as I have done for my entire life. It is not a matter of imagining from day to day the lives we *want* to live, the dreams we *want* to realize. To truly live, a man must stand and walk into the plaza, walk onto the sand and face whatever bull is there, regardless of the danger or the risk. Then he must boldly turn to then confront his life itself and face whatever danger destiny has placed before the cape he holds. It is the only way! To live and die within the plaza means transcending life!"

Fernando heaved and coughed more blood.

"Besides, I have not lost my life," he seemed to laugh. "It is your life that I have lost, Antonio. Through you, I will continue mine. With me, you die today."

"His face was growing pale for loss of blood," the maestro said. "He reached for me and clutched my hand."

"*Two promises!*" Fernando said. "Two pledges you must make to me, your brother who is at the gate! Two pledges on our father's spirit and your brother's soon-to-be departed soul!"

"A matador, I watched men die before," *Señor* admitted gravely. "I had never watched my brother, never watched myself.

"The blood in miserable Fernando's bosom had become a sticky pool, a muted crimson in the fading sun of that late afternoon.

"Fernando! I will promise anything," I wept. "I listen with a broken heart!"

"The first, because I love you and I do not wish for you to suffer this disgrace," Fernando groaned, "a vow on all things sacred: first swear to me that you will never tell a soul our secret, not until within the presence of the Angel Death, or on that day that you are certain you will die."

Antonio, he hesitated while considering the consequences of the consequential oath.

"Antonio, swear it to me now!" Fernando said. "Please make this sacred vow to me on our fraternal love!"

"I bowed my head in prayer," the old man said, remembering. "I swear it."

"And second," as Fernando struggled on. "Please promise me that you will take good care of Isabella, who will be your wife."

"Of course," Antonio replied, surprised.

"You do not understand, Antonio!" Fernando moaned. "First you must know: her heart was *always* yours. I did not know it, not until our matrimony opened wide the *toril* gate, but Isabella is the bull and I—a matador unworthy of subduing her. Perhaps she is the *toro* who can never be subdued. But you must swear to me, your brother—swear that you will never cease to love our Isabella to the death, no matter how this wild, capricious bull might wound or gore your heart."

"At that, the thought of having Isabella for my wife was all that I could think," the old man mused. "Could it be true? And would I merely take my brother's place, becoming in one day her husband? Would she know me as Fernando or Antonio? But only one day earlier, enchanting Isabella was a nighttime fantasy to me that forced me to confess in prayer my violation of the Tenth Commandment. There, on one day later, she would be my wife? I was so overwhelmed by tragedy of loss, of change and fear, and so I did not pay attention to the warning that my brother gave."

"Now, you must swear it!" said Fernando, "on our love!"

And once again, Antonio, he bowed his head. "I swear!"

"Today," Fernando grunted, gasping, coughing up another mouth of blood, "today I lived. I lived the perfect day! And for this day, I thank you, dear Antonio. The price is paid, and as I die, your glory I will carry to the other side, where I will watch you as you live. When you arrive, your brother will be there to greet you and to finish our debate.

"The mantle of Antonio will then return to you. For only then will we trade places and restore the warranted integrity of the celebrated Castañeda family, and you will once again become Antonio. Until that time, please live a righteous life for me, and leave for me a worthy name. I do not know what lies beyond, but at this time, *at pangs of second birth*, I go before you to that undiscovered country that will be our future destiny."

"The priest made signs," Antonio recalled. "'For Father, Son and Holy Ghost,' he solemnly pronounced,'" as he could see the Angel of Compassion, hovering in between the mortally-wounded matador and me."

"Fernando, I regret," the weeping vicar said to me, "but there is little time. I must anoint him so I can perform the final rites. Antonio must make the journey to a better place. Today, his name is written in the scroll of life, and we can only pray that we should be so fortunate on that appointed day the angel comes for us."

"I stood there silent, watching as the somber cleric prayed while he performed my final rites," *Señor* remarked. "The spirit of my brother left his body, with anointing oil on his head. He died on April third, the day the sun once died.

And when the crowds within the *tendidos* realized that he was gone, the wailing rivaled the inaudible Euryale, and sadness overtook the plaza from that moment on! Beyond the bullring and Baratillo Hill, the multitudes, the people of Sevilla, all the working men and wives, the sons and daughters, widows and the orphans— they began to gather and to mourn and pay respects for grand Sevilla's soon-to-be immortal hero who had fallen on that day: Antonio Castañeda de Castilla.

"I cried as well, although not solely for my brother. Selfishly, I mourned for my own life, the heart and soul Fernando stole from me when he assumed my death. The executioner of justice and divinity, Fate punishes the proud and arrogant.

The oath sworn to Fernando was not necessary in the sequel. As I watched the throng of men and boys lift up the body of my brother and to carry him about while followed by the crowds, I realized how I was loved by all the city of Sevilla and in all of Andalucía. Fernando knew. How could I, after this, how could I ever tell the people of the fraud that we had perpetrated on that day? My name, Antonio, and then the name of my own family would be disgraced for all of time."

The old man lifted up his glass. "Again, it seems our wine is at its end. Another bottle then, a third?" he asked while nodding toward his steward standing there.

I sipped the precious wine remaining in my glass. *Magnífico!* "Another bottle of this rare indulgence? Port from 1870? Indeed!" I answered eagerly.

"The city of Sevilla was dismayed," he said, "as well as the entire state of Spain. The world was shocked. I did not know my death would have a sad, emotional and profound effect on anyone. One hundred thousand candles in Madrid!

"Within one hour, I received a phone call from *Señor* Francisco Franco, hated tyrant, ruling over Spain. He offered his condolence for the loss to Spain and family, and he at once officially proclaimed three days of mourning in the nation. Yet the order was unnecessary—all of Spain would weep for seven days and more, and in the south of France, and Mexico and all of South America. Can you imagine how it felt for me? To see my death lamented, celebrated, even consecrated by so many millions in the world. It was the honor of my life!

"Entreated by the government, I traveled with my brother's body as it lied within the casket from Sevilla to Málaga, next from Ronda to Madrid, Córdoba, Castellón, from Barcelona to Valencia and to Pamplona, then to Alicante and returning to Sevilla for the burial. It was a humbling experience. I cried as did no other at my funeral, to hear the virtue of my life extolled by heads of states and fans and many other celebrated people I admired. The greatest grief, however, was despair that came upon the realization of the irony: that while so many evidenced their love for me, I never had experienced or learned to love myself."

The gentle, kind Morisca brought a red embroidered handkerchief and helped the maestro wipe his eyes and nose. She rubbed his shoulders and his back to comfort him.

"I lingered at the graveside many hours after witnessing the workers lowering 'Antonio' into the ground, and then for many hours after all the shoveled dirt was packed atop my final plot of earth," he wept. "There were so many things I wished I could have changed about my life, although it was too late for me. My life was done, and yet before me was a life remaining to be lived, a life entrusted to me by the counterpoint to my own soul: Fernando, dead to take my place."

He bowed his head in seeming prayer.

"At last I realized that I, Antonio Castañeda de Castilla, could no longer be," he sighed, "and I accepted I would have to carry forth the fortunes of my brother. I would live the balance of my days imprisoned in a counterfeit existence, trapped within the role of understudy and forever cast a deeply flawed protagonist. There in Sevilla, I was forced by Fate to finally embrace a destiny for which I was not born to live."

Tercio de Los Corazones

"And by the time the funeral was done," *Señor* Antonio said to me, "I had decided I would take up then the life of my dead brother called Fernando and would live that life with dignity and honor. I would leave for him a worthy legacy. With Isabella, I would seek a blissful, rich existence, full of quality and simple joy. This meant abandoning the fame and public adoration that I knew when I was called Antonio. Recast as second-born Fernando, I would share a private life with Isabella who would be my spirited and lovely wife.

"Before I go on with my tale, Morisco, I'll admit that I felt properly concerned and ill at ease as I approached the home of my departed brother, since after all, to take up then his life would mean perpetuation of a fraud on Isabella waiting there."

"But Isabella would have known that you were not Fernando!" I contended. "I myself know twins who are identical, yet I can differ them apart by how they talk. Yet Isabella was Fernando's wife!"

"I cannot speak for other twins," he answered me, "Fernando and myself, when devious *ninitos* playing games, we made it practice to exchange our places all the time. We made it sport to fool the gullible. And after practice, we had learned the trick of going back and forth as one another.

"Naturally, I had to learn the tone and tenor of his voice. I mimicked his inflections and his choice of words and the expressions on his face when he would speak, as he did mine. When we were boys, it was great fun, the thought of getting by with it, and we most often did, as there were weeks at times when we would fool the world—our parents and our sisters too!"

"Well, maybe," I said, skeptical. "You could not possibly have known what he would know about his home and habits there, and not about the private conversations he would have with Isabella, not about the form of intimacy they shared. She clearly was intuitive and smart. I do not understand how you could fool her easily."

"When you are twins and are identical," he said, "the world and people in the world provide surprising aid for such a ruse. All one really has to do is to remain a mute, while asking leading questions. *What did we do...? What did I say...? When did we go...? Where did we decide...?* And people, without thinking, then provide the necessary answers. Yet... I do not know that day if I was good enough to fool my clever Isabella, since I never got the chance."

"Ah, she discovered right away that it was you?" I laughed.

"No," he answered me. "Remembering my brother's death, perhaps you did not think it odd that she did not attend the funeral in honor of Antonio, whom Isabella did not know was her own husband lying there. Yet many people thought it strange, including me. I thought that she would come to be beside her husband, there beside Fernando for the funeral, but she was unavailable. I never saw her once. According to my sisters, she preferred instead to stay at home.

"And so, as I approached the house of Isabella and Fernando for that tense initial *rendez-vous*, I was perplexed about the reason that she did not come and equally concerned that she would see right through my ruse to take Fernando's place. The sequel would inform that I had worried needlessly."

"So she *was* fooled?" I interrupted, curious.

"At first I thought she was," he said, "but how is one to know when dealing with a creature who, innately born, is cunning and so clever as a woman is? When I arrived, I saw that all the things she owned were packed in luggage, standing by the door. And Isabella stood beside them, there with two young boys, while waiting anxiously to speak with me. When I approached and came into the dining room, she sent the boys away and called me to the table where she sat."

"Fernando, I am leaving you today. I have two reasons," Isabella said. "The first of those: because you are a liar, yes! And *adúltero*! I have learned about your wealthy student, this Veronica! She came to see me, telling me that she was worried over you. So bold, yet so naïve! A silly girl! It was not hard to force her brave confession. You told her that you did not love me, and you never had, and that you married me because you were resentful of your brother, and you only wanted to deny Antonio a happy life with me. How you are such a petty man! And now Antonio is *dead!*"

While sitting there," he sighed, "I could not make an answer, so remaining silent, I seemed liable. I could not know the recent situation in their home, though I would think, *not good*. But she continued, rage and anger growing as she spoke."

"*¡Cabrón! ¡Vete al carajo!*" Isabella yelled. "I told Veronica that she could have you for herself. I do not want you anymore. For your convenience, I sent her home and told her to retrieve her things to bring them to this house, to make a life right here with you. You wanted her? So there you have her! She is in the bedroom, waiting for a life with you."

"But wait!" Antonio complained. "Please, I am innocent! I do not love this girl. I do not even know her. I love you and only you!"

"Oh, save your declarations of affection!" Isabella sighed. "Just save them for your silly girl. Perhaps this little tart will be impressed by your appeal for longer than I was, but on the other hand, perhaps she will become a woman and desire something real. But it is good for you that there will always come another crop of simple-minded girls into your celebrated university. You can impress them with your knowledge, which will not be *good* for poor Veronica. I told her in my gypsy voice: *Veronica will be betrayed!*"

"Veronica has lied to you!" Antonio objected. "Bring her out at once to face who is accused. I do not love her and will tell her that. Have faith! Believe me, Isabella—I love only you!"

"Oh really? Even in the many times you spent within her bed?" she asked. "Your sweat combined with hers? Your body breaching many times between her open thighs at intervals throughout the night? You lie! She told me *everything!*"

"But I am injured by a fraud!" he groaned. "Believe me, please!"

"When I was just a girl, then I believed. I am a woman now, and women *feel*," she said. "The difference is profound between a woman and a girl. It is one thing to catch the fancy, fascination and imagination of a silly girl, but quite another trial to win the intricate and complicated heart belonging to a woman who has known the heat of passion in her life. When I was young, you captured my imagination, but Antonio, he snared my heart."

"*Antonio* snared your heart?" he asked, surprised. "Then why did you not marry him?"

"Because I was a girl, and you impressed me with your great ideas and fantasy," she answered. "Your appeal was to my mind. Romance is of the mind, and so reality can never stand against ideal, but love is of the heart. As just a girl, I was not capable of understanding this, as only women know the ways of love."

"And did you love Antonio?" he asked.

"Yes. From the moment that I met him," she confessed, "I loved him. As a girl, I did not understand the sacred duty that I owed to love, and so I chose with mind instead of heart."

"I want to know. What duty did you owe to him?" he asked.

"But only one," she said. "It is the highest duty, which is truth. And so, Fernando, for your lack of diligence to truth, I cannot rest another night within the false, imagined heat of your cold fire."

She struggled to hold back her tears, which sought escape from reddened countenance and eyes. She wiped her face and set her jaw and grieving eyes in opposition to his own.

"Antonio, he was a matador. He was a man who lived and loved a life of passion, unlike you. He understood his spirit and the spirit of the bull, and he engaged it," she explained. "A matador must know the place wherein the true heart lies and so he seeks to *know* the heart. Fernando, you will never understand a woman and will never love, be loved or yet experience love because you live within a fantasy of mind, outside the heart. You never faced a bull, not one."

She clutched her hands and wrung them, cringing in regret.

"Yes, I forgot my duty," she continued, "since I should have told Antonio I loved him from the start. I chose against my heart, betraying love and truth! I should have told him that he was... was father to my oldest son, my Josélito standing over there."

My writing and recording stopped. *How could that be?* "But wait, *Señor!*" I called in protest. "How bizarre, this twist of fate! Did you just say that Isabella told you you were father to her oldest son? And did your brother know?"

"I don't believe he did, Morisco," he explained, "but one can never really know the simple truth without distortion when a woman is emotional. I did believe she thought she was revealing some great secret to my brother. But for me, I did not know I had a son until the very moment she confessed. And what a shock it was, remembering we were together one week only in Madrid! One week, and after that, I never saw her face again."

"It's true," she said with greater confidence. "*Antonio* and I enjoyed expression of a mutual love and intimate companionship when he was in Madrid. Your brother was intensely passionate! He took me to the plaza where he fought three bulls and dedicated ears and tail to me before the people as a public declaration of his love. That gesture and his words were something to remember and a special gift that no one else, except the finest matador, could give. I loved Antonio with all my heart!"

"And never once you told him this?" he asked.

"My situation would not let me speak. I married wrong and where I did not love," she sighed, regretting, weeping. "You are weak, Fernando, without balls, "forever hiding in your books! You cannot understand injustice when it means to love someone so much—yet disallowed unfaithfulness by sacred vows—to be forbidden to express the truth."

"Regrettably," he said, aggrieved, "I *truly* understand."

"But now," she scoffed, "because your vile adultery with Veronica has rendered spoken vows and promises without effect, I am no longer bound to you. Connubial duty has returned to my own heart. I am divorcing you. If I were able to defy both death and time to find Antonio and marry him, I would, but he is dead."

She wiped the moisture from her face and stood, prepared to leave.

"I want a man who lives, and not a lily-livered man who thinks and who imagines things, who merely *talks* of things he wants to do and places he would like to go. I cannot live without the passion I deserve! I want a beating heart and heated blood!"

"But Isabella!" he declared, "I am that man! I live! My heart still boils, spilling forth my love for you! I understand!"

"Stop now!" she argued then. "You fooled me to believe you understood to merely pacify your wife! You promised you would love beyond your faculty and swore that you would face one bull for me to prove your love. But then what did you do? What have you done? You took a whore. Though she is young and very pretty, she is nonetheless a whore."

"As God will judge," Antonio affirmed, "For all this time, I never was unfaithful. I could never love another soul!"

"And for that lie you will receive the *judgment of Onan!*" she loud pronounced in gypsy language with malevolence. "Veronica has showed me proof! And yet it is no consequence to me, for I have found another man, a matador, and one who loves me and will gladly claim the prize that you have thrown away. His name is called Romero Sánchez. I will be his wife."

"Romero Sánchez?" he exclaimed. "I know of him! He is good-looking and well-bred, but as bullfighters go, he is a circus seal who swims with hungry sharks—a simpleton, forever lacking style, and creativity and *love* from those who watch and understand the art. He is a solemn man, severe and fearless, though a lousy matador."

"It does not matter," she replied. "He is a matador, and any man who fights, who cares to risk, no matter how unskilled or feeble, he is better than the man who will not dare to fight at all."

"And do you love this man? I asked," he said, "because I knew then where her heart did lie."

"Again, it does not matter," Isabella answered, "since I know Romero is a decent man who does not fear to live, and that is all I ever wanted in a man. No, he could never be Antonio, but he comes closer to Antonio than you."

"If that is what you want?" he asked, "Then I will fight a bull for you! Or up to seven bulls! Tomorrow, if you like!"

"Fernando, you cannot succeed enough to fight two bulls," she said. "*The first fight you can win, yet you will die upon the sand before there is a third.* I think you cannot hear, Fernando—I have told you this before! Do not forget that I have gypsy blood!"

"To hear her speaking so, I grew more desperate," he said. "I would have said or offered anything to make her stay. I looked into her eyes and hoped that she would be reminded of the week we spent together in Madrid."

"We made such passionate love!" he said. "Please look into your heart or look into my eyes. Perhaps you can remember me?"

"Remember you?" she sighed, "For making love? *¿Estas loco?* My appetite was ruined by Antonio. No one could satisfy me after him. You are a shower to a hurricane.

"Until this day, you have not fought one bull, though you are capable. When you consider risk, you are afraid and take your place within the stands. Without a daring heart, you are incapable of love. How can you love me when you cannot even love yourself?"

"I tried to take her in my arms," he said, "I said to her, 'please come with me, and let me show to you how passionate I am. Let me make love to you!'"

"Ah, passionate?" she tisked. "Come! You were never passionate! Why you were boring in the bed I realized, it is because you do not own the bull within, and that explains why you have never given any of the bull to me, not like Antonio. A life of passion only was a dream for me, but I awakened from that fantasy and left the bed.

"Perhaps Romero, who is but a matador of little means and consequence, perhaps this man can give my life a small degree of passion and excitement, so I can endure until I grow so old that I am good for nothing in this world. *My story ends in tragedy!*"

"As always, Isabella had a flair for the dramatic circumstance," he said. "She wept a moment there before she summoned for the boys and then the servants of the house. I bowed my head in sadness, realizing I had lost her for a second time. The situation was impossible! To shy away from telling her the truth would be betrayal, but to tell the truth would be an even greater infidelity!

"And once again, my heart just seemed to burst when all that I could do was look into the heavens without gladness, calling, '*Why?*' For certainly, there had to be a reason for so cruel a fate! '*What is the meaning?*' Sadly, when I looked back to the place where she had stood, my Isabella was no longer there. I was alone again."

"But what about Veronica?" I asked. "I thought that Isabella said Veronica was in the bedroom on that day?"

"Ah yes," he said. "Veronica, another episode! Yes, she was there, but she was not in love with me. She loved Fernando. She adored her teacher at the university and did not want a bullish matador. She wanted someone intellectual, a boring thinker. After Isabella and the boys were gone, Veronica emerged quite timidly, afraid that I would be exasperated after Isabella left."

"*Veronica?*" I wondered, speaking to myself. "What did she look like? Was she pretty too?"

"Yes, it was obvious that bluish, noble blood was running through her veins. Yes, she was very beautiful. In fact, I was surprised to find that she was that same pretty girl who stood before the class to share with me and everyone the things Fernando taught—the same who made comparison between the bullfight and the love affair between a woman and a man."

"And yet another irony!" I sighed. "This same young woman—in his home? But did she think you were Fernando when she saw you there? When you were in the class, did you perceive a clandestine relationship between Fernando and this girl, while you were teaching in his place?"

"No, not at all," he said, "and for that reason I soon realized that she had lied to Isabella, or perhaps in discontentment, Isabella, without reasoning, accepted what was most convenient to believe in order to provide escape, to leave a marriage to a man she did not love. So I believe Veronica adored Fernando in a fantasy, but never in a sexual relationship."

"What happened next?" I asked.

"She came out slow and cautious, studying me at first," he said, "a cunning creature. First, she bowed her head and told me how much sorrow that she felt for me because my brother twin, Antonio, was murdered by a bull. By then I knew that she was testing me to see if I was angry over her deception. Knowing this, I did not give her what she wanted, but instead, I used my grief to hide my heart, though not in sorrow for Fernando's death. Instead, it was an anguish yet again for losing Isabella to another man."

"I'm sorry that your wife has now abandoned and betrayed you in this time of great unhappiness and woe," she said. "But it is obvious to me she did not love you anyway. She said that much and more to me while you were gone. She said she always was in love with this Antonio, your brother. When he died, she realized that life with you was all a lie, a counterfeit. She said that you, a meager twin, a mediocre copy of Antonio, had ruined her auspicious matrimony, making it a monumental mockery of love."

"And what is love to you?" he asked. "What does it mean?"

"It's loyalty," she answered. "After all, where is there love when there is lying and deception? Love must believe all things. It does not question, and it does not doubt. Love does not go away when temperature and passion become hot or cold, returning only in the tepidness of resignation. While impulsive, Isabella was a good and decent woman, although she, with misplaced loyalty, has never been a faithful wife to you. She should never to have married you. She never did appreciate the man you are, not as I do. I love Fernando loyally, with all my heart. That is the only duty that I owe to love."

"Then as she stood before me with her soft, consoling palm against my prickly face, caressing," *Señor* said, "I understood at once just how exquisite this young woman was, so delicate in every feature. Ah, her tiny lips—while trembling there without embellishment, were softly pink and tempting, rivaling the greatest work of Goya's hand. There was a special quality about her eyes that intimated nearness to an angel. Yet her shoulders, waist and hips were shapely and petite, her limbs were lithe. This girl was pretty in an innocent and twinkling way—not beautiful, not sparkling as a jewel the way that Isabella was... a gossamer butterfly compared to feathered dove."

"Of course," Veronica explained, "I confessed my love for you to Isabella. You may hate me if you do not love me too, but what I told her is the truth!"

"But did you lie to her?" he asked, "and did you tell her we were having an affair, when you and I both know that we were not?"

"I did not lie, but yes, I did deceive," Veronica admitted, sad, "but Isabella was so willfully deceived! Yes, I allowed her to believe what in her heart she *wanted* to believe, since it is true the heart deceives above all things. The heart is desperate and wicked, and who can know its thoughts? Yet Isabella begged to *know*, and I did not deny, though neither did I truthfully confirm her reckless and expedient suspicion. Isabella never wanted you, since she has been in love always, for all her life, with this Antonio, who in her heart will never die. Love is the greatest matador of all, defying even death."

"My heart is broken," he despaired, "as I love Isabella more than life itself. I do not know if I can walk the sands of Earth while knowing she is lost to me again. I too am lost. I do not know my way beneath the darkened sky."

"But I am here to light the way," Veronica consoled while taking up his hand. "With all the love that Isabella felt for your departed brother, I am loving you that much and even more. Fernando, I have loved you all my life, from girlish innocence transforming to the womanly conversion of my heart. You told me several times that discontent from Isabella caused her cruelty to you and made you miserable.

"You said your disappointment made you understand the real importance and the meaning of true love. You said that, given opportunity, you would discover for yourself a love still more profound than this enduring love of Isabella and Antonio. You held my hand and said... *we could embrace that love!* Upon that hint, I came and told unhappy Isabella that I loved you with so great a love. But that is what I thought you wanted me to do!"

"And what do we do now?" he asked.

"Please love me. That is all I ask, though I will never try to be a substitute for Isabella. I will only be the best Veronica that I can be, and I will love you as no other girl could ever love you, to my final breath."

"Her arms were all about me. She was sobbing, pitifully," he said, "so desperate to find acceptance deep within my cold embrace."

"Please understand!" she whispered. "I have given everything to be with you! My friends, my family! My parents have invested hope that I will wed the first-born son belonging to the wealthy Duchess in Madrid—one crazy in his head to have me for his wife.

"Fernando, I could never in my life commit my heart where passion is not there, could never be untrue to love. I swear to you that any life and love I knew before has dimmed to darkness, and I have become a moth who flutters frantically beneath a moonless, starless sky. You are the flame I seek. So singe my wings if you are cruel, but you are all I see and fly toward."

"Now I," he told me, "I was at a loss for what to think. This beautiful young woman weeping as she clung to me! Veronica believed with all her heart she was in love with me, though I could never be the man she loved, not if I even wanted to. I felt revolted by the convoluted fraud that held me in her clutches. I was trapped, and there could be no hopeful ending for us in this tangled web.

"I saw it: Isabella would forever love Antonio," Señor explained, "who for all purposes to all the world was dead. And this Romero—foolish man to marry where he was not loved—Romero would become a wretched soul when finally, he realized the truth. And yet unknowing, Isabella spurned the man she truly loved, a man who hid a painful secret, victim of an oath, a man who suffering, bore silently a secret, though his heart was being crushed again. So Isabella left for me this pretty bauble as a compromise."

"Ah, poor Veronica?" I asked. "She was in love with you?"

"Veronica believed she was in love, but I was merely an impression," Señor added, "of a man she thought she knew. The man she hoped to love was dead and gone, where in his place there was deceit, a perfect copy, who could not reciprocate her love."

"And you?" I asked.

"I was the worst of all," he sighed, "alive and dead, besieged by Fate. My heart was barely beating, and my soul was aching, yearning for a toxic drink that only made my thirst and misery still more profound. My Isabella gone, I was alone again!"

"Veronica was there," I urgently reminded him. "What happened after Isabella left?"

"'Make love to me,'" Veronica besought me then, "'for you and I will both feel better only after you make love to me. You need me now, and I need you. Two separate paths will merge as one today!'

"And after that," he said, "her slender hand slipped upward on my thigh and found its mark. Her grasp was firm, her fingers wrapping round. And leaning close to me, her fingers sliding, simulating, then she said to me, "My mouth can play much sweeter music than my hand, as I am practiced with this instrument."

He bowed his head and seemed to blush to think of it.

"I nearly did succumb to carnal reasoning," he sighed, "since after all, I was forlorn for having lost dear Isabella for a second time, and with the knowledge that, on both occasions, she was still in love with me. Both times, her mind betrayed her heart. And yet the tempting invitation of Veronica was vexing to resist. I pulled away from her, since I could only think of Isabella and the hope that she eventually would see the fraud and realize the man she left a second time was me, *her love Antonio.*"

"Veronica?" I asked *Señor.* "She gave up everything. It must have devastated her and broke her heart when you rejected her?"

"I begged Veronica to give me time in order to allow my grief an adequate retirement," he answered me. "I slept beside her in the bed, though I did not indulge myself or her in pleasures of the night. I must admit, however, it was wonderful again to have a body warm and close, when in that vulnerable place, between awake and sleep, between the light and dark, between my life and death."

I continued writing as he spoke, uncertain whether I should interrupt to ask the many questions on my mind. "And did she help you take your brother's place?" I asked, "and help to fool your colleagues and your students at the university?"

"Because Veronica was helping me," he said, "because she was believing in my grief, she never once suspected I was ignorant, and that I had no thought of how I should proceed to teach the classes of Fernando at the university. She volunteered to be my teaching helper, and so basically, she taught the classes in the way my brother taught, while I became the quiet student of his surrogate."

"Was she a good instructor?" then I asked.

"An excellent teacher!" he maintained. "Veronica learned well from all the lessons that Fernando brought. In fact, she was his most beloved student during all the time that he was there. She taught the art of fighting bulls with such a passion, and with appetite that rivaled any matador that I had watched within the ring. Veronica inspired students, challenged their abilities. She recreated and subdued their way of thinking—mine as well. Then while at home and by my side, she would continue lessons, teaching me."

"Incredible!" I thought, and said, "To spend such time with her? So pretty and intelligent! And you continued sleeping in your brother's bed with her—in order to disguise the fraud?"

"I did," *Señor* admitted then. "With every night that passed, our bodies became more and more accustomed to the movements of one motion for the other, and our sleeping styles were synchronized down to our very breaths. It was a *zambra* every night, a slow, affectionate *bolero* in between the soft and ruffled sheets, our movements sometimes conscious with intent, at other times spontaneous by sensual interpretation lying there."

"It seems there was a passion fire burning," I observed. "Eventually, you did made love to her?"

"I did not finish," he complained. "Yes, there was passion, but my mind was too distracted with the thought of Isabella, having her again within my arms. I thought in envy of Fernando's former life, though Fate had doomed me to Fernando's life in mockery: he married Isabella, had her as his wife in bed, while only as Fernando was Veronica in love with me. This girl was beautiful and bold, and intellectually, the match of any man. And then to have her in my bed at night, so soft and smooth, her silken garments cast aside!"

He paused and wagged his head, uncovering some time-obscured regret, a purposely forgotten thought.

"I could not bring myself to taking, having her," he said. "I was imagining to be in bed with Isabella, plying in her female wetness and her warmness, many times at morning and at night.

"I had become obsessed with Isabella, and so at last I quietly dispatched a childhood friend who also was my brother's friend. I sent him to Madrid to tell me how my Isabella fared, to know what she was doing there. The news he brought—it gored my heart and pierced my spirit through. It broke my hope and made me finally accept and slow embrace a self-identity that I resisted since Fernando died. It changed me so that I became at last my brother. I will tell you now, Morisco—I became Fernando on that day."

"What did your friend reveal, *Señor*?" I interrupted eagerly. Was Isabella dead? Was there some tragedy?"

"No tragedy," the maestro answered sadly. "Worse! He told me Isabella married in Madrid Romero Sánchez and that she and her two sons had then become his family," he said. "He told me Isabella seemed content. He said she told him that her love for this Romero transformed her, 'made her put away from mind all thoughts of pitiful Fernando, the adulterer, 'Fernando and his twin,' unnamed by her.' He said that Isabella would not even speak my name!"

"And you were devastated by that news?" I asked.

"That very night my heart and arms sought out Veronica for comfort," he admitted. "There always was a sensual tension there between us, like a violent river. On that night, it broke above its crest while streaming to that place where all such rivers end, into a sea of passion. For the very first occasion in our bed, I kissed her soft and trembling lips. I lingered, savoring the essence of her open, yielding mouth, so warm. My hands slid from her shoulders, down her back to find a firm and shapely *derrière* to grasp and squeeze in order to compress and hold her lower body close to mine.

"She moaned aloud at introduction of the lance and she did not resist it or retreat from it when being prodded by it slowly and repeatedly. She only pressed her body closer, nostrils flared, her pelvic movements countering my own, and thus the dance began. She panted wildly, grunting loudly, almost growling while persuading me to segue to the next maneuver with intensity."

Señor sat back while sipping at the ruby-colored port.

"In life I have enjoyed the women by the hundreds," he explained, "or by the thousands—maybe more, and so I know the body of a woman, from the tiny bud to opening to glorious blossoming. Within the next arousal stage, I properly prepared her senses and the rhythm and intensity of processes, transforming her from girl into a nymph or goddess. With my hands, my nimble fingers gently pressed, caressed at entry to the dam. And with my mouth and tongue I gauged the stream that raged and mastered its intensity and flow. My tongue, a deftly situated *banderilla*, drove her to delirium, inspiring her to speak provocative expressions and to say some things to me that I cannot repeat to you.

"Then finally, and after all the danger and deception, blood and passion, flesh and spirit, heart and mind, both she and I were ready for *faena* as we readied for the *estocada*. When at last the dance was over, then she signaled her submission in the offer of her heart. Of course, a woman has two hearts: the one that beats and thinks within her chest, and then another influential heart that pulses in a place within her loin. I plunged the sword into the second of those hearts and thrusted deeply, poetry in motion, with great style and art. Her passion was extreme, and only matched by mine. It was a conquest that I never would forget, and yet when it was time to consummate the act, I could not give to her my seed, *mi espíritu*. I spilled it in a place outside her heart.

Remembering *Señor's* description of the night of love he had with Isabella, I was curious. "Okay," I asked. "How many times?"

"I must admit that I was out of shape," he laughed. "So only twenty-five, I think, with passionate Veronica that day."

"And did you over time," I asked him, "did you after that begin to fall in love with her?"

He winced, uneasy as he plundered consecrated memories.

"To my regret," he answered me, "I never did, though actually I wanted to. I could not love her for two reasons: first that Isabella still and always dominated in my heart, while leaving me no place for other loves. I bonded deeply with Veronica because I knew her heart. She was a dedicated woman—in fact among the best that I have ever known, but never could I love her at that time.

"And that transports me to the second cause, which was regrettably continuation of the fraud. The passion of Veronica felt powerful and real, while mine seemed counterfeit. While she was honest and sincere, I couldn't be the man who she believed I was, as I was something less. I had become Fernando, but I did not measure up to him because my life was mere pretense. And yet the man who she had grown to love was more than who Fernando was, and more than both of us. I knew the end would not be good, but for the time, she brought me something that I needed, as I did the same for her."

"Yet you were lovers? For how long?" I asked.

"Three years," he answered me, "and during those good years, we were as close as any souls could be. We woke together, making love. We went to work, where at the school, I was the one who learned. We went to local markets and we cooked and ate exquisitely. And then we would debate each night on the significance of sacrifice and on the meaning of the lives we live, then on the art and essence of the bloody fight. Eventually, I overcame my bookish ignorance because I understood the meaning of the actual fight within the ring, the matters of the heart. When finally, I learned the spiritual, the intellectual, anthropological nature of the taurine arts, the matters of the mind, then I became at last complete—*el verdadero matador*."

"I see," I said. "With all the time you spent together, I imagine that she was in love with you?"

"She thought she loved Fernando," he asserted, "yet she never knew him, not within her heart the way that I had mastered it. So yes, I know she was in love with me, the man she learned to know, the man who filled her emptiness each day. She only was imagining Fernando was the man who dominated both her hearts."

I scrolled back several pages in my notes and read aloud a line I copied earlier.

"I see a problem here, *Señor*," I ventured then. "You said Veronica insisted earlier that she could not be false to love? And yet for three entire years, the whole affair was just a fraud? You said she was intelligent. How did she never figure out the lie?"

Remorseful, shameful, sad, the maestro bowed his head.

"She did," Señor regretfully admitted. "And upon the tail end of Veronica's discovery was my own stubbornness, as I for all that time refused to give to her my spirit. For that time, when after I was satisfied, then I withdrew my sword. I spilled my seed onto the ground always, outside her pounding second heart, or yet into the *cintas*. And for that, eventually I felt the horn."

"But why?" I asked him. "Why not give to her your seed?"

"Because I was to her, 'Fernando,'" Maestro answered me, "and any child she bore would be his child and not my own, a fraud from birth. The lie would be continued then into a future generation. As if affairs were not already over-complicated! Pregnant with a child, Veronica would want to marry me."

"Why not?" I asked, "Why not if you had truly taken on your brother's life?"

"From that first moment that I touched the hand of Isabella," he remembered then, "and from the first occasion that I felt her warmth, her energy—then I was drawn to her the way in which a careful and selective hummingbird is drawn to his specific orchid flower in the canopy, which God created just for him. So I could never give myself completely to Veronica as long as there existed *hope* that I would someday have my Isabella in my arms again. I longed for Isabella, my eternal sun within the sky, to end that night of tragic fate. Still it was barely after noon. Still there was hope."

Señor Antonio, he paused to wipe a tepid nagging tear that hung upon the corner of his swollen eye, though it was followed by another, larger still.

"While Fate caused me to take my brother's life and to forfeit my own, no force of heaven or of earth, no entity of flesh or spirit could remove the love of Isabella from my heart."

Touched by his unintended though emotional display, I paused a moment and proceeded, candid, to my next remark.

"Then I feel very sorry for Veronica," I said. "This was not fair to her. How could you let her fall in love with you, when all along you knew you never could return her sentiments. How cruel to her, *Señor*! You owed it to her after three entire years! Of all the people in the world, she would have understood!"

"Remember—I had sworn an oath to the departing spirit of Fernando as he died," *Señor* Antonio explained. "He made me swear it on his soul and on the soul of our dead father. What was I to do?"

"Well, if you could not tell her that you really were Antonio," I dared, "then why not let her know that you could not return her honest love?"

"Morisco, you must understand I tried to love Veronica. I tried to make her happy," he admitted. "So when Isabella left, I thought that I could make my way in moonlight, as so many do. But when I heard that Isabella married this Romero Sánchez and forgot my name, then I believed the warmth and brightness of Veronica could fill the void, could light my skies. I swear I tried to love Veronica! I even told her that I did one time, but mine were empty words and weightless to her heart. It was those words, when finally, I said them to her face... that caused her to suspect the fraud."

He stared again into the glass, remembering his past.

"By then, almost four years had passed," he said. "Yet over twelve declining months before, the warmth and sweetness of her voice, her words and temperament had changed to cold and vinegar. This was because she wanted children, so for every time I spilled my seed outside her heart, for every time that I refused to fill her yielding body with my spirit, it would seem that her resentment grew."

His wrinkled face showed indication of the desperation that he must have felt while sharing such a personal experience with me. "Then she would ask me, 'why?'" he said. "Why I would not bestow my spirit to her heart? And she would weep and hate herself for being undeserving of a child, of love and marriage. Many times, I tried to reassure her otherwise, but words provide their proof in evidence. And once she tried to still her broken heart by opening the veins along her wrists while in a bath. By accident, I found her and I pulled her from that awful sea of blood and misery.

"But after she recovered from her self-inflicted wounds, she never was the same," he said. "And from that moment on I knew that she was watching me. Veronica, she studied me and my demeanor, analyzing everything I said in order to discover if I would betray my heart and oath."

"Why?" she said one day, "Why is it that you told me many times before I came to live with you, that you had never loved the brooding Isabella, calling her 'a worthless prize?' Yet *now*, you pine for her as if you never said those words to me at all? The very sound of Isabella's name—that name makes weak your knees so that you swoon and almost fall upon the floor whenever Isabella's name is called. I *see* it now! Why did you tell me when my heart was young and supple that you held a tender love for me and *never* her! You swore to me you loved me then. And so I gave my youth to you. *¡Hijo de puta!*"

"But she had just begun," he said.

"You *think* I am that same naïve devotee that you fooled three years ago?" she scoffed. "You *think* my eyes have not begun to see beyond or through the aging cape you twirl? That day in class, that Friday afternoon, when you wrote on the board *derecho*, with your right instead of left? You *think* that I do not remember that? And those romantic conversations in between us that are presently unknown or absent in your memory? The wine together and the poetry you read? The possibility of children and adventure? The content of the books you wrote with your own hand, so foreign to you now? And when you said to me before, 'I love you'—*Now* I ascertain those words came from another heart... another man."

"She closed on me," he said, "a woman as a beast, an agile creature, dangerously a *serio*, and she was cutting off the ring so there was no escape, her bearing dangerous, portending death."

"You meant it..." she insisted, "yes, you meant you loved me when you were *Fernando*. Now I must believe that he is *dead!*"

"No!" he protested. "Still I *am* Fernando, standing here!"

"You dare continue such a lie!" she threatened him. "I do not know the why or how it happened, but somehow the man that I and all of Spain saw die in glory on that day upon the plaza sand was not Antonio. The man who fought that fiery, infernal bull, *Muerte*, three long years ago, was actually Fernando who, within his broken heart, who truly loved Veronica! Fernando died for you, and you committed fraud on me and fraud on all of Spain! You are Antonio! *¡Ladrón malvado. Ai!* You stole the sacred carnal sacrifice I offered up to him in love. You stole my alter gift!"

"Without a weapon, I continued backing, dodging her as she approached," he said. "She was relentless while pursuing me."

"Why do you lie with me? And why do you deny the truth? Your sexual greed consumed my innocence for three whole years! You spoiled my virginity!" she screamed while lunging, scratching at my face with fingernails. "You took a virtuous girl and used her as a concubine, but I become a woman here before your eyes, and you will pay for your deceit!"

"Then on the second pass," he said, "she viciously attacked again, but I reacted, tablecloth becoming *el muleta* as I led her, grasped her wrist and spun behind her, causing her to trip and tumble to the floor."

"But you lied also, fraudulent Veronica!" he shouted. "You were in the bedroom when I came because you *lied* to Isabella! Yes, you told her we were having an affair, a lie injurious to innocent Fernando, who was slandered by deceit! You told me what you did. Your lie is why she left, the reason that I do not have her now! You are a victim of your self-incriminating treachery."

"If I had not been here, you would have lied to Isabella!" out of breath, she growled. "All men are overgrown and foolish little boys. To think that lying is the way to overcome a woman's will! Do you not know it is impossible to fool a woman in the matters of the heart? If Isabella truly loved Antonio, she would have known you when you came! But face the truth today: *she did not want your vulgar and deceitful ass!* You lied to me and then you used my body for three years. Now you must pay in pain and blood!

"I thought I knew her," he explained. "I danced with her at first, and yet I did not truly calculate the danger of a woman scorned. I did not see the veiled *puntilla* there, the curved and shining dagger in her hand, until the moment that she hooked and buried it into the flesh beneath my ribs, just on the left, identical to where Fernando had been gored, except for on the other side. In shock, I looked down as the knife came out and blood began to

flow. She had intended for my heart, but she had missed. *¡Ay!*
¡Pinchazo!"

"*Now Die!* Antonio!" she hissed. "*¡Muérase! bastardo egoísta!*
My Fernando was a better man than you! Fernando *loved* me, loved
my heart, a heart that you destroyed by fraud! You wounded me
beyond a cure, and now I've wounded you! Now shame on you,
Antonio! And when you see your brother on the other side, then
you will have to answer for your callousness in using me. I love you
and I hate you all at once! Love is the cruelest sport of all!"

"She left me there to die," he said. "And if not for the gardener,
who saw Veronica while leaving with the bloody blade still in her
hand, I would have died that afternoon and you would not be
sipping such extraordinary wines tonight."

My writing stopped. I sat amazed by Maestro's nonchalance
while sharing such a poignant memory. "And you were taken to the
hospital, no doubt?" I asked.

"They had me in the hospital for over thirty days," he answered
then. "They said that my sinistral lung collapsed. My body bled so
much that doctors thought for sure that I would not survive. They
closed me in a room and pulled the curtain shut and sent a priest
to give the final rites, but it was not my time to die. The angel knew
but was detained by matters in the Spanish Civil War.

"And that is when I learned why I had lived. You see, my heart
was different, unique. Because I am a mirror-image twin, created in
reverse, my heart is on the right and not the left as it was meant to
be. Veronica had found her mark and missed because she did not
know my heart and where it lied."

"So it was on the right? Incredible!" I interrupted. "But
Veronica? Was she arrested after her attempt to murder you?"

"Veronica was not," he countered then. "I paid the gardener
for keeping quiet while I told *Policía* that robbers, *los ladrones*,
came into my home and stabbed me as I fought with them."

Señor Castilla took a breath and sighed. "Veronica departed to
Madrid in order to repair her wounds with family. Although we did
not speak, we had an understanding. She would not reveal my
fraud, and for my part, I would not tell authorities she tried to
murder me."

Unbuttoning and opening his shirt, he showed a heavy-
muscled chest, and leaning to one side, he then displayed the
ancient keloid scar.

"The most extraordinary memory of my life with volatile Veronica exists on this persisting wound that I still bear, the only time I ever was severely wounded by a bull."

"Did you regret not telling her the truth from early on, considering the way that things turned out?" I asked. "If you had life to live again, Señor, you would have *told* her, yes?"

"No, I would not," Señor explained. "I do not have regret for anything that I have done all in my life. While there have been disastrous circumstances, some involving pain, I've found that these were needed lessons, and I call them gifts of love from God above, if one lives long enough to understand and to appreciate the point.

"This scar is just a physical reminder of a lesson learned. Veronica—she left her mark on me. Yet in the end, she gave me what I needed to move forward to the next experience. She gave me something necessary, vital to my living and my growth, and I believe I gave the same to her. The life of man is far too short to dwell upon regret. When all is said and done, I've learned that everything that happens, happens for a reason so that in the sequel, as we age, then every reason is potentially a lesson to be learned."

"I must agree. And after you recovered from the injury," I wondered, "you went back to teaching at the university?"

"Of course," he answered, "By that time, I learned to love the art of teaching. I became more comfortable with living as Fernando even as we merged identities. As I grew more complete, I realized I had become a better-focused, better-dedicated teacher than Fernando ever was. His students had become my students, and his colleagues were my own, while I was loved by everyone. Yet there was loneliness, of course, while living as a counterfeit, and so I filled the time with studying, consuming books, becoming educated at philosophy, biology, world politics and literature in seven different languages. I even wrote a book about *corrida*, which included one extraordinary chapter that detailed a famous bullfight long ago between *Muerte* and Antonio Castañeda de Castilla.

"Perhaps one year had passed," Señor continued, "when a grandee passing through Sevilla told me that Veronica had gotten married to the wealthy son of royalty, and she was living in Madrid. He said Veronica had then become an elegant, distinguished woman of society. The news was pleasing to my ears, as I wished nothing but the best for her. However, there were times I missed

her, times I longed for her shrill voice and for the sweet, familiar
fragrance of her breathing when the morning came, her soft caress
as we exchanged a kiss while passing in the hallway in the
afternoon, the flutter of her heart so close to mine at night. I
wondered if she missed me much the same."

"And after two more years," he sighed, "dear Isabella wrote to
me and told me that she craved to bring the boys to visit me, here
in Sevilla, in my family's home! I naturally and eagerly agreed. To
see her face again! Six years had passed, yet I was as a teenage boy,
imagination racing, my emotions on the edge, at conflict with
myself. I bought new clothes. I had the house remodeled and I
brought in fresh-cut crocus flowers from La Mancha—this because
I knew she loved the delicate effusion of the honeyed saffron in the
warm and slanted springtime sun. That much was written in the
journal of my brother, who had made extensive notes about his life
with her."

"I also made exquisite preparations for the boys," he said. "I
first arranged a special visit to *El Torre del Oro* and a trip to *La
Maestranza*, for a private exhibition. The older boy was called a
nickname from my father, Josélito, and the younger for his father,
Fernandito. If you remember, Isabella told me, or she told the same
to counterfeit 'Fernando,' just before she left—that Josélito was my
son, the son belonging to Antonio! Yet how could I believe? She was
an angry woman, and such women often tell cruel lies to wound,
abuse or cause regret, so I was cautious in believing what she said.

"They came upon a rainy day in early spring, upon a day it
seemed the very sky was cracking and was falling, all in liquid
pieces, down to earth. The wind blew hard, the sounds of thunder
boomed, and then the darkened sky flashed eerily, florescent white,
with godly scrawls in streaks of light across a tapestry of grey-black
clouds.

"A taxi brought them shortly before noon, and by the time
they got into the house, their clothes were positively soaked. The
boys put on dry clothes and warmed themselves beside the fire
while their mother, Isabella, took a steamy bath."

"She figured out the truth, and she came back to tell you that?"
I guessed, but he ignored the question as he closed his eyes.

"I noticed right away the suitcases were tattered and were old,"
he said, "the same that she had left with six years earlier. The pants
and shirts belonging to the boys were faded and threadbare in

places, though the clothes were clean and neatly-pressed. Their hair seemed tousled and their stained and crooked teeth required dental care. Both seemed to have forgotten that my house was once their family home, or else perhaps they grew accustomed in Madrid to scarcity and were uncomfortable with having servants and abundant luxuries. I offered then a little wine to make the boys more comfortable.

"I think that Josélito had twelve years, or thirteen maybe, while Fernandito must have had then nine or ten. I did not know precisely what their ages were, but they reminded me of my dead brother and of me. The older was defiant and refused to be intimidated by the house or anything he saw. His only interest seemed to be the many pictures of the bullfighters and bullfighting that hung inside the trophy room. The younger was reserved and shy, and he preferred to read a book in quiet contemplation in the peaceful, flickering light before the fireplace."

"It seems you like *corrida* and to follow matadors?" he asked the older, who inspected with attention and concern those photos of the greatest bullfight of all time.

"I do not merely like *corrida*, mi **Papa**," José responded, arrogant, impudent too. "I love the bullfighting. I *am* a matador."

"I laughed," *Señor* explained, "though not to mock the boy. 'A matador? You are so young!'"

"It does not matter. I have killed eleven bulls thus far," young Josélito answered, "yet before I die, I'll kill one thousand bulls."

"Where did you learn to be a matador?" *Señor* then asked.

"At *La Escuela Taurina de Madrid*," the boy responded. "Yes, the finest school for bullfighting in all of Spain. And when the people learn of me, then I will be the greatest matador the world has ever known. I wish to live and die just like my celebrated uncle Antonio Castañeda de Castilla."

"I cringed to hear those words," the old man said, "though in the same way I was taken by surprise when Josélito called me 'Papa' for the first time in my memory. I looked into his eyes where I could see the flame that burned in me at thirteen years, the hunger for unrivaled glory and success—that same testosterone-generated insolence. If even Isabella had not told me so, I would have known this boy, this Josélito, was my son."

"This school that he attended—was it good?" I asked.

"It was the best," *Señor* assured me. "One must spend a fortune to attend this school, and so I asked the boy, 'Who paid for your expensive training?' knowing in advance that unremarkable Romero Sánchez, toreador in poverty, was husband of his mother, Isabella. Following the gossip from Madrid, I knew the clumsy amateur had fallen down financially."

"I have an unknown *patron*," Josélito said. "My mother's nemesis has publicly assured Madrid that it is you, my father, paying for the school to sponsor me—but you would not reveal yourself because you do not wish to humble and disgrace her husband, an inferior torero, who has neither money nor the patience to indulge ambition in a son belonging to another man."

"Of course this hidden patron was of news to me," *Señor* admitted. "During all that time, I had not heard from Isabella, so I did not know what happened with the boys, what passions and whatever inclinations they adopted or inherited. But I was not surprised the older, Josélito, loved *corrida* and he thought that I had sponsored him at this great school? It was not me!"

"And so you never knew who sponsored him?" I asked. "Did anyone?"

"No., I did not *deny* that it was me," he said, "but neither did I dare confirm. And even now, Morisco, I can only guess."

He sighed, determined to continue his account.

"When Isabella came out from her bath," he reminisced while smiling, "she was beautiful—a flower to a shoot from six years earlier. She was averse to kiss my cheek on seeing me, as it was custom then. She seemed more flushed with color, seemed more ripened as a woman then, absent the laurel green and tart unfinished edge of youth. Her years were thirty-two perhaps, or thirty-three at most. She wore a robe, and yet from stolen glimpses as she moved about, I reconstructed what was underneath. *Dios mío!* Isabella was more beautiful with age. The fruit had ripened and was opulent.

"I offered her *jerez*, a light-styled *fino*, which of course, is sherry wine, and we dismissed the boys and took a place before the fire they surrendered, seeming in complicity with her."

"This is a lovely place," she smiled and said, "and yet how many hot and steamy nights did you indulge your passionate affair before the flames with this... Veronica?"

"Veronica is gone," he said. "What does it matter now?"

"Veronica is nothing other than a whore!" she said and seemed to revel in those words. "She lived unmarried with you as a strumpet for three years! But in Madrid, she tells the world she was your dedicated student, nothing more, and ever chaste! And so she wed the first-born son belonging to the Duchess and pretends to honor noble blood. All this while in Madrid she makes life difficult for me and your two sons! Two *times* this year, she took great risk and obvious expense to mock me and humiliate me in the eyes of those whose powerful respect I spent five years to earn! And intuition tells me that she makes the elevation of Romero difficult, and so my husband cannot rise to higher prominence, and so he must continue at the plaza fighting bulls while he is past his prime."

"I have not seen or spoke with her for many years," he said. "Veronica is of no consequence to me."

"As we spoke more," Señor went on, "I wondered if she would suspect the fraud, as Isabella was, by all accounts, intelligent and shrewd. She always was intuitive. But in that moment, just as in the moment when she left before, she had allowed the heat of angry blood and thinking of her mind to overwhelm the better sense of wisdom in her heart. And on that first occasion, when she chose Fernando over me, her mind was stronger than her heart. Fate was a teacher who was using irony, derision and adversity to shape my life. *I stand before you, Isabella! Your Antonio—the man you love, who loves you as the sea the shore!* I felt her heart reach out for me, but to her purpose and her state of mind, I was invisible."

"She lied!" then Isabella sneered. "She was in love with you! She lived with you for three entire years! Now you must tell me all, so then I can destroy the fraud she lives! Did you one time seduce her in your bed, in order to devour and enjoy the whoresome pleasures that she offered you? Fernando, answer me!"

"I did not want to answer such a question," he confessed, "but not because I was ashamed. I would not lie, and yet I thought it useless to provide for Isabella arms and ammunition in a hopeless battle that she probably would never win.

"And so I told her that I did not 'one time' take Veronica into my bed, and that was only half the truth, because I took her many times, a hundred times, or perhaps one thousand times. Dejected, Isabella seemed to be defeated by my answer, so while sitting there she did not say another word. She stared into the flames, her mouth pronouncing silently concession, anger and regret.

"And that is when I understood why Isabella came. At first, I hoped it was because she longed for me and she had realized the fraud, but that was in my overworking heart, which got the better of my mind. And then I thought she came because she wanted for the boys to visit with their father and for me to know my sons.

"But as she sat there, listless, staring at the flames, I realized that she had come to gain the ammunition and the arms from me in order to destroy Veronica, to spare her husband, this Romero in Madrid. She wanted to exploit me, once Antonio, though in that moment I was just a pawn to her to gain her selfish end! I saw through her deception, and at once, I was incensed."

Señor, he then withdrew a knife from leather sheath and started cutting from a block of sheep's milk cheese from Ronda. Then he sliced a large *blanquilla*, called a 'Spanish pear.'

"Before they came, I took some money from the bank in order to provide support for Isabella and the boys," he said. "I do not now remember what amount I took, but it would be approximately fifty thousand dollars in America today. I placed the heavy leather satchel in her lap and spoke but looked away.

"You have received an answer, though not what you hoped to hear," he said. "And I regret that I, Fernando, am not helpful to your purpose. I am not some ignorant, inconsequential, meaningless *novillo* to be played for sport! You are dismissed! Now take this money for the boys and crawl back to that amateur Romero in Madrid. I want no more of you, so I will have a servant drive you to the station so the train can take you home."

One of the woman servants, the Morisca, after watching *Señor* struggle with the hardened rind around the cheese, she sat with us and rescued *Maestro* from the knife. She subsequently placed a bowl of dates between us on the table and she left.

"And after telling Isabella she should go back to Madrid," he said, "I swore I would *renounce* the sun and all its light and follow in its stead the moon, the planets and the stars in ignorance. Six years I waited, hoping Isabella would one day explore her heart to find me there—Antonio, the man she loved! Yet this was my reward? To be inconsequential, a *peone*—and this time in sport for women fighting over vanity? Again, I said unto the sun: *Why this? She cannot see or feel Antonio? Why cannot Isabella, of all people, not discern the fraud? It made no sense! By order the heavens would I be forever in the dark!*

Then Isabella called my brother's name as I forsook the fire and the light, but I had left and did not even turn to answer her."

"That was the end of things with Isabella?" I inquired.

"To my surprise, she did not leave," he said, "but she continued there in silence for a week, attending to the household chores and duties as a seeming wife at home. It was as if she never left. She rearranged the furniture in order to increase the flow of *chi* into the home and then she went to shops in town in order to replace old art with new, contemporary art."

"And for what purpose was she doing this?" I asked while interrupting. "Did she realize at last you were Antonio?"

"I did not know," he answered me, "and yet I took advantage of the time to spend it with the boys. I helped the younger, Fernandito, in his studies of the Latin language, his declensions of the nouns. I made a failed attempt to help the older, Josélito, with his form and then his passes as a young torero in the ring."

"A failed attempt?" I asked.

"He did not want my help," the maestro sighed. "He did not mean to mock, and yet he told me I was not a matador, that he instead should teach good form and fearlessness to me."

"You know philosophy and such, but you have never faced a bull," young Lito said. "You've lived your life while hiding in your books and teaching what you do not truly understand. So you could never know what it would mean to be a matador, a man who lives a life of passion—who is hero to the world. I'm sorry. You are not Antonio, my uncle who was loved."

"I then became intrigued," the maestro said, "and so I said, 'But when the angel took your uncle, you were very young, a barely-weaned *niñito* still. You really do *believe* your father's brother, dead Antonio—he was a hero then?'"

"Of course I do! He was the greatest matador to ever live!" my son replied, "and he was loved by all the people here and everywhere. By measure of his life, I know the man and matador that I aspire to become. I would have loved my uncle, but because you hated your own brother to the end, I never got to see his face."

"My eyes were filled with tears while hearing Josélito speak," *Señor* reflected, hiding agony. "Of hate and love! I grieved to think that 'hate' and 'brother' followed in that sentence spoken by my son. To hear young Lito say he loved 'Antonio,' while yet his heart was far removed from me as spurned Fernando standing there! I wanted to confess the truth, yet I remembered then the oath I promised to my brother, who I loved, and could not find my voice." The old man wiped his eyes and shook his head.

"And do you not respect your father standing here?" he asked the boy, "a *scholar* who has undertaken study in philosophy and higher things, whose written words have earned the admiration of the world and elevated all of Spain?"

"You are intelligent, Papa, and I am learning too," the boy responded. "But we both must know that learning does not happen at a school. It happens in the head, within the mind. And schools exist for those who have not learned yet how to learn. That is the only teaching worth but one *peseta* at a school—the only subject that a school can teach. The scholar learns but does not live."

"And that is all?" his father asked.

"No. I respect you as the world allots respect," the boy sustained. "Because you have *pesetas*—then your *wealth* commands esteem. And yet without your means, my father, you'd be just another scholar in an ignorant world where underprivileged scholars are denied respect. I know that much.

"And yet the bullfighter inspires awe. To fight a bull requires strength, but you are weak. You hide in books and buildings, far away from life upon the sand. You have allowed my mother, who was merely angry for your sin—you let her leave you for another man, a false, dishonest matador who then abuses her and your own son. Antonio, my uncle, would have never left my mother to the base, indecent appetites belonging to the wealthy in Madrid. A father worthy of respect would not forsake his proper wife and sons. Until the day I die, you'll not have my respect!"

"Without a further word," the old man sighed, "unhappy Isabella and the boys were packed to leave when morning came. To my surprise, and while the children waited in the taxi—Isabella, she returned to kiss my cheek and then my mouth. The kiss was brief, but it contained more passion than I ever knew until right then. My heart was stilled and did not beat for several seconds. That is true! Has such a circumstance befallen you, Morisco? Have you lived a moment where you loved someone so much that for an instant you were numb, your unremitting heart completely still and silent in its place?"

"Ah yes," I answered, almost weeping, my heart aching. "Yes, I have! Teresa was her name. A pain like yours I have endured. I thought that I would die!" I closed my eyes a moment to compose myself. "Did Isabella stay?"

"The choice was neither hers nor mine to make," he said. "On that occasion, we were victims of our fate. She was a wife whose husband waited in Madrid. So after that distressing kiss, I saw a sadness in her eyes that I had never seen before. I thought to grovel at my knees while begging her to stay, but when she seemed to sense what I would do, she turned her back and walked away. Ten paces in the distance, then she turned toward me again. And she was weeping as she said to me, 'My darling, *be yourself*. Forget me if you must, but please, be who you are!'"

"What did that mean?" I asked. "She figured out the truth?"

"I did not know," he said. "But after hearing Isabella and the heavy words of Josélito, I had changed. I took a leave of absence from the university in order to assess my life. I wanted to go back to what I was, to what I loved, to feel again the sand beneath my feet, to smell the sweat and taste the blood of bulls, to feel my very arteries while straining, ready to explode in danger and excitement, two desperate hearts that balance back and forth! A dance so delicate and perilous. O how I wanted that again!"

"As who? Antonio, or as Fernando?" then I asked aloud.

"As Fernando Castañeda de Castilla, naturally," Antonio insisted. "It could be no other way and was not easy. It required five full months of vigorous exercise in order to regain my previous form. And still, the first time that I practiced with a bull, ¡Ay! ¡Paletazo!— a blow from flattened part of horn. It knocked me to the ground, and then the bull, he came for me and barely missed my head by kicking with the hoof. He gave to me a deep and painful bruise directly on the ribs that took two months to heal."

"How old were you?" I asked. "What is the ideal age for fighting bulls?"

"My age I think was thirty-two or thirty-three," he said, "so I was in my prime, yet I was out of practice, lacking confidence. It was one-thirty, maybe two. The sun was high in early afternoon."

"Did you begin to fight the bulls again?" I asked.

"I had to start a *novillero*," he responded, "this because the world believed I was my brother, who had never taken his *alternativa*, or the graduation for a *matador de toros*. I had paid for Josélito to return, and so he was *padrino* at my ceremony.

"My first contest, I had to fight a huge *castaño*, who was petulant and hated man, but I prevailed, and I continued, winning many contests in Sevilla and in all of Spain. In two years' time, the people came to love me and to celebrate my name, while some believed that I possessed the resurrected soul belonging to Antonio, the greatest of all time. Excited to return, I danced as I had never danced before. I loved to be there in the plaza, feeling hearts, as many men and women lived their lives through me. And women! Oh, a star, a moon, a planet every night! And sometimes two... or three! And everywhere the women—they all wanted me."

"A matador—your life is like a rock star, yes?" I asked.

"More like a star in sports," he told me. "Like a player in the NBA, like Miguel Jordan—I think he was a Bull. Or like the baseball MVP. And every night real women, those of quality, they came to me—not like the cheap, beer-drunk, drug-crazy women of the rock and roll. The women who I dated, they were lawyers, doctors, teachers, heiresses and royalty—who were respectable, who knew that there is nothing better than true passion in a man, who knew there is no man who has more passion than the matador."

"And did you fall in love?" I asked.

"Oh, every night!" he laughed, "And sometimes many times within one night! But I avoided married women, though I could have had them. All except for one. One married woman mastered me and took advantage of the sin and weakness in my heart."

"A woman? Who?" I asked. "Who was this woman then?"

"She was a woman of influence in Madrid," he whispered in a lowered voice. "She always watched me from a distance so that she might find me on occasions when I drank too much. Then she would send a surrogate to me, seducing me. Of course, when at the end of this seduction, yet before the passion and before the making love, she then would switch in places with the surrogate, and I would take her in the darkness, but I always woke up to an empty bed. On only one occasion I awoke in early morning light to see her face before she left the bed and slipped away."

"So who?" I asked again.

"It was Veronica," he said, "my former nemesis, the same who had assumed she stabbed me in the heart, while leaving me for dead. That same Veronica! And when I looked into her eyes, she smiled and turned away and left and never spoke a word. I should have known her in the dark, as it was unmistakable the way she touched and moved, the way she danced with me. I think my instincts were not fooled, although the thought was inconceivable."

"She had a husband?" I confirmed.

"The first-born of the wealthy Duchess in Madrid!" he said. "I was convinced she hated me, and I believed that I would never see her face again, and so to realize that she would risk her reputation, honor and her marriage in exchange to spend those sensual sexual nights with me! I was amazed to see her there."

"You never found out why?" I asked.

"I was perplexed for months," he said, "but finally I realized, at least in part, the reason she was there. It taught me how to truly comprehend a woman's heart."

The maestro nodded, indicating to Luis, who brought a bottle, crystal Baccarat—of Remy Martin Louis XIII, along with three cut crystal cognac glasses.

"Let us finish with the port," he told Luis. "Then we will entertain the angel when he comes!"

"Most men will never understand," he said to me, "but to a woman, passion is a drug, a potent drug that can affect the heart profoundly, given opportunity. Most women live their desperate lives without a single moment knowing passion—hunger, as it courses through the veins and arteries, the elevated senses and lightheadedness, the powerful intoxication!

"Once a woman has experienced this, she never will be satisfied with less, regardless of the risk. This woman realizes that in life, that passion is the only worthwhile thing. It is the fire and the fuel that heats the blood, so in the end—once she has eaten of the fruit, her eyes will open. She will seek it at all costs, and even at the risk of everything she knows."

"Veronica experienced passion earlier with you?" I asked, "and not in married life?"

"It was so sadly obvious," he said. "The woman who has felt and tasted passion learns to understand and tame the beast that lies within the heart of every man, for purposes of pleasure. If there is no beast that rises to the sport, then there can be no sport, and so no passion there. This woman will not go without for long or live unsatisfied. This passion will become addiction, and the woman, she will crave and find excitement elsewhere, often in a former lover—with a beast she knows."

"I think I understand," I said. "But you said passion was a drug?"

"Yes, for the woman, passion is a potent drug that stirs the heart," he said. "But not so for the man. Within the man, the passion lives. It breathes and feeds. It is the beast that lives within his heart. It is the animal. It growls, it throbs and rises up within the soul. And always hungry, with voracious appetite, it seeks to hunt and to devour woman flesh. Unfed, it weakens and it dies. Most men will never please the woman who has learned to crave adventure, danger and excitement. If he has trained himself, he can at best control the ardor and rage of this wild animal. And yet the woman maestra can subdue the beast."

"The woman maestra?" I inquired. "I don't understand."

"The man is matador beneath the sun," he said, "the woman—matador beneath the moon. He leads at day, but she will always rule the night. When making love, within the passion of the dark, it is the man who has the horns—at night the woman holds the instrument of fate. Beneath the moon and stars, the woman always has control, though she may let the man believe he wields a potent sword. But this is part of the deception and her dominance.

"The woman tempts with the *muleta*— tempts with what she wears—the presentation of the well-formed legs, the pretty feet in shoes that tease the eye, the slender neck and supple breasts; the way she smells—her personal perfume, the mesmerizing, irresistible effusion of the oozing female body pheromones that drive the beast to near delirium (although it knows not why).

"How she presents herself—the painted lips, the painted fingers and the toes, the scarlet skirt that clings onto the curves of slowly, soft, gyrating hips, the silky smooth bare skin, and finally, the ultimate enticement of the flesh—temptation on the limb that caused the fall of man: Good to the eyes, it is the irresistible, intoxicating fruit the woman takes and gives to man. And under its influence, the man will follow as she dances. He is led as she performs *fijar, chicuelina, correr la mano, pase por bajo, citar, llamar* and finally, *suerte de matar!* He seldom has a chance."

"And that is how Veronica exploited you?" I asked.

"Veronica made me to realize at last that I was being treated as a whore. While I believed that I was taking my advantage of the many women coming in to me," he said, "in truth these women came to use me for their selfish purposes, to ride and tame the beast, to sate addiction. All the while, they treated me no better than the beast I had become. I was a senseless animal, used for their sordid pleasures and for other selfish ends. Veronica—to see her there, I realized that I had been a fool for all that time, and never did I walk beneath the darkened sky again."

"Oh what a life that you have lived, *Señor!*" I sighed. "So many trials and twists of fate! But such a life!"

"And yet I have not told my story fully through," he said. "A month had passed, one month since I discovered the deception of Veronica, when I received the strangest news. It was about Romero Sánchez, husband of my Isabella. I received a telegraph communication that Romero had been gored along the upper leg while fighting at *Las Ventas* in Madrid. The doctors tried to save him, but he bled to death while in the *enfermeria* there. There was perhaps a paragraph, or maybe two, reported by the local news— no more than that."

I sat surprised, and looking up, I spoke. "Romero Sánchez dead, you said? Romero? Isabella's husband died?"

"Romero died," Señor affirmed. "There is an ancient Andalusian saying, *Donde menos piensa el galgo, salta la liebre,* which means in English, 'things will happen when you least expect them to.' Yet I was equally surprised by this as anyone. The gypsies also have a saying: *after bad luck comes good fortune.* I did not rejoice, but neither did I mourn. I waited, knowing that eventually my long-lost Isabella would come back to me."

"I never have believed in fate, except the fate we will ourselves," I said while looking up. "It seems to me you two were being drawn together by a force, by more than mere coincidence. You believe that it was God... or destiny?"

"Yes, pages in a story written long before the two of us were ever born," he sighed. "I did not travel to Madrid to join the funeral because I had engagements that I could not cancel in Pamplona and in Barcelona. So when I went home, I found a message there from Isabella, who had wrote a note to me.

"Of course, by then, I was considered once again the best of all the matadors in Spain, in all the world, but this time by another name, Fernando Castañeda de Castilla. At that time, in my assessment as a matador, I think I was the best that I had ever been, since in this second life, I understood both parts—the heart and spirit in the ring."

"I do not mean to interrupt, *Señor*," I said, "but what about this message you received from Isabella? It was awful news?"

"No, not at all!" he laughed. "Her letter said she had a relative, a niece related to her mother, in Triana, which was not so far from me. She said that she would come to visit for a wedding ceremony, adding she would like it very much if I could come to visit her while she was there."

"Triana? Yes, I know that place!" I said. "I went there for *flamenco* and the gypsy wine."

"Ah yes," he nodded, seeming to reflect. "It is a gypsy *barrio* in Sevilla known for that, but when I went to meet with Isabella, that was many years ago, so it was very different then. The place was not as big or known by those who were not gypsies, and the people there were real, grown from the soil rather than from money of the tourists coming to that place. What outsiders peeked in and made to be romantic—this was just the ordinary life of people who were living there.

"We met together in the month that followed after gored Romero died, but Isabella went there for the wedding of a niece, who was the daughter of her cousin's wife."

"She brought the boys with her?" I asked.

"They did not come," he answered me. "The older, Josélito, was engaged—a *mano-a-mano* match, *corrida* in Valencia. His younger brother went to be a *peon*, to begin his training as a banderillero. So, no boys—she came alone."

"Ah-ha!" I laughed. "How perfect for you! (Though no doubt you said a prayer to mourn Romero's death.) And by that time, she knew you were Antonio?"

"I did not know if she had realized the fraud," he said. "I could not know. I tried to make it to Triana to attend the evening wedding, but the time was April, *La Feria*, and the *primavera* rains were still with us. It really did not matter. Gypsy weddings sometimes go for two or three entire days. I did not care about the ceremony. Selfishly, I only wanted once again to see my Isabella standing close to me."

"At last, *Señor*!" I sighed. "To have her in your arms again!"

"It probably is not what you are thinking now," he said. "When I caught up to her that night, she celebrated on a tavern patio with relatives. And they were drinking, talking, listening to gypsy songs, interpreted with virtuosic skill, this by a man whose hand was crippled, and who must have lived already sixty years or more. The slow, accomplished picking of the strings could barely be discerned above the din that filled the dimly-lit and smoke-filled area. And so I stepped inside the gate while squinting to discern the face of Isabella from the many other women who were there. This was because her aunts and cousins—many shared her likeness and distinctive physical anatomy."

"*¡El Bailarín!*" someone called out, Señor! remembered.

"Once inside, the old man on guitar, who must have recognized me from a picture or the television, he began by playing *pasodoble* music. He was playing *Manolete*, I recall. At hearing such familiar music," he continued, "music that was faster and more spirited, all eyes out on the patio were turned toward me still standing at the gateway. Ah, the *pasodoble* songs are meant to mark the entrance of the matador into the plaza ring and later, when he executes the final passes right before the kill, in the *faena* done.

"And when I looked again, the lovely Isabella stood there at the center of the patio, while posed *desplante*. What I always loved about the gypsies, or *Romani*, as they call themselves, is that they pleasure and they take advantage in the unpretentious, ordinary moments of a life: unique and fleeting moments that the rest of us, ensnared by fear of spontaneity, will let with passion slip away and wither unexploited, in the past.

"So there stood Isabella, posed with wavy hair pinned upward on her head. Her dress was more than black, but *azabache*—radiant and shimmering. Her shoulders and her arms were bare and glistened with the moistness of her sweat and youth beneath the spotlight of the moon. Her dress was long and fitted, with a crimson cape that wrapped around her waist, and with Italian crafted heels on pretty feet.

"And suddenly, the *pasodoble* ceased, and then the guitar maestro played a song he purposed for the gypsy soul. The song's beginning was a morning call to prayer in Casablanca, then the syncopated melody began. The crowd joined in with clapping hands and stomping of the feet, the slapping thighs and sometimes elbows on the tables. Isabella closed her eyes as she began to feel the rhythm of the room.

"She started, barely moving at the first, with arms raised high, her elbows bent, and snapping fingertips. The passion of the song eased down her body to expressive hands, to graceful wrists, down past the elbows to her pretty face, her neck and naked shoulders, quivering and resonating in her breasts and down along her w waist to slow, gyrating hips, deliberate and lingering down her firm and contoured thighs to legs that showed El Greco in comparison to be an amateur. She then began to stomp her feet, beginning the *bolera*, turning slowly in a circle.

"As the music quickened, Isabella danced. She twirled her graceful skirt, she spun and raised her arms while striking poses, snapping back her head while clapping loud. And then she snatched the crimson cape tied at her waist and she began incorporating that into the dance. She draped it at her shoulders and across her back, continuing interpretation of the match.

"And looking toward me, she approached, her cape becoming as *muleta*, teasing me. She dared me to indulge the *pasodoble a flamenco*. Tempted, I could not refuse, so heated I pursued the temptress as the *matadora*, while I was the bull. We danced, with one pass leading to another pass until the very end: *ajustarse, farol, recorte*, then the others on the patio began to dance with us. We must have danced for two entire hours on that floor, and then we found a table where we sat and we enjoyed the most incredible sangria I have ever drunk!

"We spoke a while as I grew bold to lean in close enough to kiss her on the mouth," he said. "And her reaction? Then she slapped my face to chastise me."

"'That slap was for the first lie that you told to me!' she said. 'It does not cover all. Forgiveness comes with time.'"

"I was surprised, and so in my reaction, without thinking and without remembering my place," he said, "I then returned the slap to her and said, 'And that was for the first lie that you told to me! You loved me, but you *used* me, then you married my own brother after that. One lie, one arrow—and the casualty, three birds, three injured souls. *Uno estoque, tres corazones*. I am not forgiven? You have wounded all of us. A second chance is rare.'"

"But I was young," she said, "and I allowed my foolish, girlish thinking and my lack of trust in love to rule my heart. When I knew better, it was then too late. But you! And that Fernando too! What was the thinking in your heads to be such fools? To toy with Fate! Your brother died, and you—Antonio, you are a fraud. And with imagination, one might then conceive pre-meditation too!

"Two brothers, fighting from the womb! The violent one, he uses animosity that grew for many years to goad his prideful, feeble brother with a point to prove—to put this brother in his place upon the plaza sand, to set him up against a supernatural bull whose name and destiny means 'Death.' He does this all to *kill* his brother and to steal his life to covet then his wife! Is this your wickedness? Was that your plan? And did you think I would **not know**?"

"There is but one who knows the nature of my heart, its subtle poetry, and that is you," he sighed. "And for that reason, I was certain you would recognize me right away, but you chose not to see, and chose—a second time—the passion and entreaties of another man instead of me."

"Why did you lie to me?" she asked. "You could have told the truth when first you came! We could have been together then. I never would have had to suffer with my sons the cruelty arising from Romero's insecurity so many years!"

"I swore an oath on my dead father's soul," Antonio explained. I swore it to Fernando and his spirit as it flew into the sky: *I promised never to reveal what we had done,*" "The whole idea of trading places was *his* fantasy! I was against it and I begged him to withdraw to let me face *Muerte*! Yet Fernando would not yield, the hazard frivolous to him! He loved you, Isabella, and he knew you wanted only for a matador. His dying was a final act of love."

"I married after him a matador," she said, "Romero! *¡Qué lástima!* It took a little time to realize the measure of a man is but the measure of his heart and has not much to do with title or with wealth. And it is not his excellent or his imperfect face that he provides the world to see. For I would love an ugly beggar from the loins of thief and womb of prostitute, if only he could understand me, and he loved me as I needed to be loved! And let the world scorn me—since I would rather revel in the joy of poverty, the wife of foul and horrid beggar than the consort of a handsome prince who has no passion or the need to understand my heart!"

"I should have recognized you then," he told me that she said as she caressed his face. "I should have known you were the only man in all my life who knew the character and weakness of my heart and mind—though not until that moment when I kissed you as I left that rainy day. The heavens tested us."

"Yet we prevailed," he said. "And after all that we endured, we are together now."

"Together, yes," she said, "and yet what lies beyond 'together'? In our yearning, did we once consider life beyond our merely being 'with each other?' Did we wonder what our life would be, together, day by day, beyond the wanting and desire of imagining?"

"For fourteen years I held my breath of life in order to breathe next to you," he said. "Unwaveringly I toiled, I tended to the flocks of Laban. I have stopped the beating of my heart to set my time in pace with yours. It is the warm part of the afternoon, and we are fortunate the wind is still. For only now we hear the music from the stands. So what to do, together, day by day? We dance!"

"But not tonight," she smiled and then she moved his heated hand that touched her inner thigh. "My Tia Azucena is a woman very strict. See how she glares at me right now! I am her houseguest, so I must return with her. But ah! The air is scented with the orange blossoms and is filled with jasmine flowers honey sweet. Tomorrow is the April Festival. So let us go to *Los Remedios* to spend a day of celebration there, and then we will decide how we begin this dance."

"I drove directly home that night as if to be reborn!" he said. "It was the grandest moment of my life, Morisco. Oh, to be united with, at last and for all time, my greatest love. Again, *imagen del espejo gemelos idénticos!*

"Within that night, I was unable to discern my sleep from wake, the dreaming from reality. In prayer, I begged of God to never wake me if it was a dream. *'Please let me die, so full of love and happiness!'* I begged. When I awoke, the rendezvous with Isabella proved to be reality, and so my prayer was not answered on that day as I remembered always, *God is good!*

"I found the lovely Isabella waiting in Triana, then we went to *Los Remedios* to see the April Fair. Three days we went to the *casetas* in daytime hours—tent pavilions for exquisite tapas and sangria all day long, and then we went to private gypsy places for the dancing late into the night, where Isabella wore the bright *flamenco* dresses, delicate, extravagant, with lace *mantillas* and her leather boots. When it was late, and after all the dancing, Isabella went with Tia Azucena. I went home. On Saturday, she wore a black *traje corto* to match my *traje de luces*, as I was determined there to fight four bulls at *La Maestranza* on that day. *Evento especial* — to master on that day *four* bulls—a sacrifice for me and for Fernando!"

"And you fought well on Saturday, those bulls?" I asked.

"Yes, I fought splendidly!" he answered. "Just before my final match, when at the *brindis*, or the toast and dedication of the bull to someone special or to yet the crowd, I asked permission of *el presidente* for a slight indulgence as a favor to my family. The crowd was quiet as I knelt and fell to both my knees, a humble man before the multitude. The trumpets blasted. I was at the very center of the plaza, audience within the stands, or *tendidos*, many more on television. Then, before the world and God, I begged the goddess Isabella on that day to marry me."

He paused to sip the brownish port, and then it seemed by his expression he would move to something else. *But no!* I interrupted him because I had to know! "Please!" I persisted. "You asked Isabella on your knees to marry you? How did she answer then?"

He grinned toward me as he returned the glass to tabletop.

"You have to ask, *cabrón*?" he laughed. "Of course! she smiled, and she said, 'yes.'"

Yet after drinking so much port, *Señor* rose slowly and he traveled to the bathroom to relieve his body of the wine which, separated from its spirit, passed onto the other side. We took a break for maybe fifteen minutes. Then we sat to talk again.

"We had our wedding at this very house, in two weeks' time," he said, "and it was marvelous, the most spectacular and stunning wedding celebration ever in Sevilla, past or present, and with fanciful, elaborate carriages, interpretive performances and Andalusian horses pulling carriages. Our wedding vows were deep and intricate professions of our love and gratitude. I dressed as Figaro, and Isabella was Susana on that day. But Isabella, she and I were keen to leave our guests behind and to begin our private consummation, which we conceived to start in Casablanca, in the very place where you were born, Morisco. On that night we flew down to Morocco, called *the land of setting sun*."

"To Casablanca? To a place so dear to me!" I said. "But you are Sevillano. Why to Casablanca then?"

"For many years, it marked the western edge of ancient Earth. I had a friend, a history *aficionado*," he explained, "who was the owner of a glorious place called *Mano de Dios*, or القدرة الإلاهية, above the beach—a villa, Mediterranean in style, that sat upon a cliff that overlooked the cold Atlantic sea. To stand on that veranda at the end of day, the sound of waves forever roaring, crashing—and the vision of the fiery, burning sun while plunging down into the deep blue, chilly sea—the vast horizon that extended out in all directions from the eyes!

"A servant there, a Berber man who called himself Bushmar—he told me that the spot was called a holy place, that always, at the moment when the sun would disappear—he said that humble pilgrims, if they turned so ever slightly, viewing from the corner of one eye while squinting—that in this extraordinary moment they would see *the hand of God*. And they would resonate, would be at one with all the heavens and the Earth. They would enjoy a moment of a rare and spiritual clarity. Yet from the first occasion I was ever standing there, I thought of sharing it with Isabella, *only after she would be my wife*."

"And that is where you went to celebrate your wedding night?" I asked.

"We flew directly into Casablanca after our reception," Maestro said. "Miloud, the driver, met us on the tarmac at the airport. So the driving was one hour, maybe more than that, beyond the city, through the cloudy darkness up the winding roads. And when at last we smelled the sea, we looked afar, and what a welcome sight was shining there! A castle! Ah! And once inside, poor Isabella sighed and wobbled, overwhelmed while standing in the foyer. Seven splendid bedrooms! Gurgling marble fountains, pools and garden squares! A palace to enjoy for three entire days!"

"A wedding so spectacular by day and travel in the night?" I asked. "And were you too exhausted when you finally were there?"

"A man is never too exhausted on his wedding night!" he laughed. "But once again, it probably is not what you are thinking now."

This time, he filled again the glasses by himself and handed me the bottle from his hand. "A souvenir," he smiled, "and given so that you remember me." And then he cleared his throat. "Ah, what is the hour now, Morisco? Do you know?"

"It is eleven-thirty now," I answered him.

"Eleven-thirty?" he repeated in surprise. "I dally way too much! What was I saying to you now?"

"You were just telling me about your wedding night," I told him, scrolling back, "how it was probably not what I thought."

"Ah yes," he said, "that is because, you see, a matador will always take his time. He never can afford to be so rushed or anxious. Isabella, she and I would be alone within that gorgeous home for three whole days, and so I planned according to the time we had."

And once again, his eyes glazed over just a little, tearing up as he recalled that night while looking back so many years.

"On that first night, I ran for her a bath. There was a huge bright copper tub within the master suite," he said, "So then I filled the steaming water with abundant fragrances, with lavender, with cloves and cinnamon, with lemon grass, Egyptian musk, nutmeg and honey—an auspicious alchemy. A flask of aged *rioja* from Álava with a glass sat on a stand next to the tub. And I had lit one hundred candles all about the room. A tape recorder played a lengthened version of *Boléro* by Ravel, set to 'repeat.'

"All while she bathed," Señor continued as he wiped tear-moistened eyes, "I carefully adorned the bed in red silk sheets, and with one thousand petals, plucked from fragrant red-black roses. After Isabella rose up from the bath, I dried her skin with heated cotton towels and brought her to the bed. And it was after midnight when I placed a silk sleep mask of red across her face and told her to relax. I rubbed her body then with olive oil, extra virgin, and with added drops of lavender for tired arms and legs. I took my time and asked for her to close her eyes and take deep breaths as I then tied together her two wrists with woven strands of silk. I turned her to her stomach, and I anchored both her wrists to the strong pillars of the bed, and then I gently bound the ankles separately to other bed supports."

"You tied her up?" I asked. "Oh no! *Verdaderamente!*

"But only for the object of adventure and discovery," he said. "The silken threads could easily have yielded to her will, but they were just enough to make her feel the sense of helplessness at being thus restrained—and meant to gently force submission of her body and her mind to purpose of my ardent quest. My lips and tongue, the travelers, were eager to begin their task to chart the hills and vales, the undiscovered coves and streams, the wonders even she had never known—in order to explore her body and to find where all her secret sensual places lied, the source of passion unrestrained.

"The foot of willing woman," he began. "What better place to start! Oh, I could spend one day or more in worship of one foot alone—the curves, the arch, the nerves, the sensitivity and pleasure found between the toes! The foot, when she has been sedated and subdued, is such a sensual place and it comes third, but only to the flower of her love and then the breasts, which resonate her heart. So I began my delicate discovery, beginning with her heels. I gently nipped at them, I nibbled at her arches and I traced design and shape of every toe with warm, responsive tongue. And all the while I felt the beast within my heart begin to rise."

He smiled at me, continuing.

"To feel the beast!" he said. "Most men will pass through life and never feel it there, will never let it rise to animate their hearts, will never bring exquisite ecstasy or passion to a single woman's life. And for that very cause, the great preponderance of men will settle into life, monotonous and uninspired—and by that effect, the vast majority of women thus are doomed to passions unfulfilled.

"For when a man completely loves a woman and has passion in his heart, he kisses first her feet. He must restrain the beast that craves devouring all at once. He sucks her toes, each single toe unhurriedly. He finds the hidden places where the secret pleasure dwells. I took my time to carefully adore her feet.

"Then I began along the edges of her sculpted ankles and her shapely legs, exploring with my tongue and lips the curves and lengths, the soft and firm expanses of her luscious flesh. I then continued biting her, but not so hard to make her feel the pain, though in a way to make her feel the vulnerable sensation of her being gradually devoured by a beast, of being craved and hungered for. I studied her as well—the way she moaned, the way she twitched and quivered at my slightest touch."

He closed his eyes while savoring the moment long ago.

"The soft, forgotten place behind her knee, her thighs, her hips—I took my time to kiss and to caress. And then her back! Do you not know, Morisco, that a woman's back is sensually a pleasure map to be explored, with carnal joys beyond her reach? And Isabella had a smooth and supple back. I trailed my tongue along her spine and beastly breathed behind her neck, the nape, and then I kissed behind her ears. O how she loved the kissing of the neck! It was as if I flipped a switch to "on." She moaned aloud, so physically aroused, and grinded with her hips! The silken strands that bound her wrists and ankles strained against convulsions in her shoulders and her legs. But being patient, then I stopped to let her body settle down."

"You stopped?" I asked.

"For but a moment," he responded. "Then I turned her to her back, still tied at wrists and ankles, and I then began to suck again her toes, to slowly work my way from feet to neck again. But it was getting late. I did not touch the flower, though I flittered near about until I passed and licked her stomach and her waist. I lingered on her breasts and feasted as a hungry newborn child until I had my fill. I kissed her neck and then her mouth and held her body close to mine until she begged for satisfaction. That is when I stood, and kissing her goodnight, untied her from the bed and left the room."

"It was your wedding night!" I criticized, unhappily. "You left the room!"

"I did," he said, "as it was one of three full days and nights that we would have there at the villa. For a first, it was a stimulating and adventurous night. So after leaving, I confined myself within another sleeping room and locked it as I closed the door."

"And Isabella?" I inquired. "Was she happy on her wedding night to sleep alone?"

"Well, no," he laughed. "She was not pleased at all. She stumbled down the stairs, along the hall. She stomped and cursed a little—words, expressions I am sure she learned while in Madrid. And she was banging on the walls, demanding that I must return, but I was tired. It had been a long, eventful day. She pounded on the door for maybe thirty minutes more and she made many threats, but then eventually, she went away. And thank the heavens! I was tired."

"I'm guessing she was no less angry in the morning?" I surmised.

"Her bags were packed!" he laughed. "She tried to leave, but we were on a high, steep mountain, many miles from nearest neighbor or a town, and we both knew Miloud would not return the noon. She let me talk her out of leaving with a feigned reluctance. We were sitting there, within a grand and sunny kitchen. She was cursing me while I was making breakfast. After she had spent the better part of her emotion and the food was on our plates, I asked why she was mad."

"It was my wedding night!" she screamed. "You persecuted me. You filled me with desire, tempting me, seducing me, and then you made me spend my wedding night alone!"

"But you were not alone, as I was in the house," he said. "Besides, already you have had two *other* wedding nights. This final nuptial and tertiary wedding will prove different."

"On hearing that," he said, "she, with her forearm, shoved the plates right off the table and she did not eat one bite."

"Why? Cruel Antonio?" she criticized as she began to cry. "Why would you tease your wife to leave her unfulfilled?"

"Ha!" I interjected, looking from the pages I was writing when I thought I understood. I asked Señor, "but isn't that exactly what she did to you while in Madrid? She tempted you and left you for Fernando after that. You wanted her to know the heartbreak that *you* felt?"

"Not true," he said. "I told her that in order to make love to her as no man had, then it was necessary to discover and to understand her body as no one had done before. I told her of the secret pleasure place I found behind her neck and of another spot at left above her waist, and of another on her back above her hips and of a place upon her scalp. I kissed behind her ear and whispered, 'Ah, my love, how difficult it was for me, like Phineus, to have a sumptuous feast spread out before me, yet I could not eat!'"

"You were so cruel!" she said.

"But only to be kind, to love you better," he returned.

"Let's get this straight, Antonio!" she differed. "I am not a bull!" You cannot lead me where you wish for me to go."

"Of course not," he agreed. "I am the bull and you are maestra. So where you lead, then I will follow you. Where does my master wish to go?"

"My wife was quiet," he recalled, "suspicious, scheming in her head, and finally she spoke."

"Hah! Shopping!" she announced. "I wish to shop, and you— for what you did to me—will pay! Yes, you will pay! While under normal circumstances, I will buy my own or go without, but after what you did to me last night, you have to pay!"

"I understand," he said, "so I will call to have the driver come for us as soon as possible. The Old Medina is a splendid place to shop!"

"In Old Medina *is* a splendid place to shop, *Señor!*" I said while sipping from my glass, "since it was not a month ago when I was there!"

"Especially so when we were there," he answered me. "She purchased lamps and spices, copper curios and rugs and tapestries. She bought Moroccan clothing for the boys, *djellebas* and *babouche* slippers for their feet. She purchased silver bowls and serving plates and an elaborate brass table from the merchants there.

"Oh, Isabella loved to shop!" he smiled. "Three hours passed, and she had bought so many things that, even though she packed them carefully, the car was filled. We could not fit inside the limousine with all those things she bought, and so I sent Miloud back to the villa by himself to take it all up there. I asked him to come back for us, but he had other obligations that would keep him occupied for hours. Nonetheless, he said he knew a taxi driver who would take us back and told us where this man would always park.

"And by the time we finished shopping more, I heard the stomach of my Isabella, roaring like a lion, grumbling and complaining for the lack of food. She begged to eat, but I insisted that I could not trust to let her eat the food down there. She was my wife, and I was loath to see her sick all night in misery, and so I bought for her three tangerines, which she consumed with grunts and groans. I promised her that I would cook for us when we returned to *Manos* on the hill, and so we set about to find the taxi driver who would take us there."

"Yes," I agreed, "she must have been so hungry, since you left Sevilla in the early evening on the day before and she destroyed her breakfast earlier. She hadn't eaten for how long? Almost a day?"

"She ate the tangerines," he shrugged, "and then a little taste of cheese milk from the goat. Well anyway, we found the taxi and I paid him well to take us back to *Mano de Dios* on the cliff, but when we reached the bottom of the hill, he stopped the taxi and he told us that he could not take us any farther up because his car was lacking brakes."

"It is not far from here," the driver said. "It is three miles, or maybe four. Believe me! *Allah*—blessed be his name! *Allah* would punish us—three fools who tried to travel up and down that mountain without brakes!"

"And so he left us at the bottom of the mountain road to walk," *Señor* Antonio said. "And when I checked my watch, already it was after four. '*Ay-yi-yi-yi!*' I told her then. We had to make it back to the veranda of the villa by the time the sun will set! We have to see the hand of God! And we would have to walk four miles, and steeply up the hill. My struggling Isabella—she had bought still other things, and so our arms were full of bags. I set a quick and steady pace, and she kept up perhaps one quarter of one hour, then she sat and said she needed rest.

"I worried that the sun would set, so I encouraged her to hurry with some firmness," he explained, "since at the pace that we were traveling, we would not make it back in time. Oh, she was panting, breathing hard and tired, angry, having conversation with herself. I think she may have slept a little in the night before—two hours, maybe more, but I continued with encouraging words. 'Please faster, dearest love, we must go faster still!' I said to urge her on.

"And by the time we got to halfway up the mountain, then we heard a rumble in the distance, not too far away. It was a heavy rainstorm, coming right our way. And what to do? We could not go back down, and it was two miles up to reach the house, with no one and no neighbor in between. There were some trees for shelter, or there was perhaps a cave, but with the storm, the dark was coming as the sun would set. 'And there are animals about, perhaps a lion or a leopard,' I advised, 'since after all, we are in Africa, with hungry beasts about. And then the rain began to fall."

"We must walk faster still, my love," he said, "if not—the rain might wash us down the hill, or worse. Walk faster, please!"

"How has it come to this, Antonio?" she screamed through tears. "Was this your plan? To trap me out like this? To wear me down? Why have I married you?"

"You credit me too much, my love," he said. "I could not plan a storm! And it was you who wanted to come down to shop. I only want to get you back to safety. I am walking. You must keep a better pace with me. You have no choice."

"There always is a choice," she countered. "Yet you do not credit me enough!"

"And then we walked another two miles up the mountain in the cold and pouring rain," he spoke. "And as we went, one of the rain-drenched bags began to tear and broke apart so that its contents crashed onto the ground and slid back down the hill, and then a second bag. So by the time we reached the villa, there was only left one pouch that held a silver *koummya*, this a Berber dagger she had bought. Our clothes were soaked, and we were frozen to the bone."

"Was Isabella right?" I asked. "Was that your plan? To wear her down with lack of food and sleep and warmth? Much like Petruchio?"

"The matador does not rely upon a plan," he said. "He feels life with his heart, the bull in all of nature... Well, perhaps I had a bit to do with what the *driver* said, though you must know I did not cause the rain that we endured."

"I'll bet that by the time you finally had made it to the villa, Isabella thought to use that Berber blade on you!" I volunteered.

"The thought did cross my mind," he said. "Though actually at that point, I think that Isabella was just happy to be safe and warm, as it was quite a journey and adventure that we undertook that day.

"To my surprise, we made it back to the veranda just in time to see the sunset, but the clouds were covering all the sky. The storm would rage throughout the night, the thunder booming, etchings of the lightning on the tapestry of nighttime sky, a symphony of sound and nature! In such moments, we, like Job, will learn humility. Our troubles and the trivial ambitions of our lives meant little in the greater scheme of things. The sky, the edge Earth and then the hand of God were not intended to be seen that day."

"Oh, what a shame!" I sighed. "Was Isabella angry with you, when you, after such a struggle in the bitter storm, you did not see the hand of God?"

"Initially, and for the first few moments, yes," he said. "Not after she could see what pains I undertook to make her comfortable. I made a raging fire in the hearth. I gently dried her hair. I took her rain-soaked clothes, replacing them with cozy, warm pajamas, woven from the softest wool in all the world. I also wrapped her in a plush, embroidered cotton robe, imported from Afghanistan. And sitting on a couch before the flames, I took her tired, blistered feet into my lap and I massaged until her eyes began to roll back in her head. When finally she was asleep, I made the most exquisite dinner I have ever made, her favorite meal."

"And what was that?" I asked.

"*Paella*! Yes, you know *paella*," he asserted. "I had asked Miloud, the driver, earlier, to search the markets all along the ocean, and he brought for me the clams and mussels and the giant prawns, the *calamar*, the fish, the rabbit and the garden vegetables, the olive oil, *bomba* rice and finally the most important spice of all, the honeyed saffron threads. I cooked it as she slept and woke her to a feast."

"I'm sure that she was hungry after such a day!" I said. "You served her dinner by the fireplace?"

"Yes, I had set a table there," he said, "with fancy plates and linens, fine Tunisian wine and the traditional Moroccan bread. She gobbled down the food at first, but after she began to feel the meal, she slowed and smiled toward me."

"And what is now in store for me tonight?" she asked. "Will I be robbed and ogled by the handsome rogue Aladdin? Maybe *Ali Baba and his forty thieves*? Abducted by the wicked caliph so that you will have to start a quest to rescue me? Or will this villa slide into the ocean, leaving you and me to brave the tossing seas to find a perfect island paradise? So come with it, Antonio! Bring on adventure then, *El Bailarín*! Your movements I have learned. Tonight, I am prepared for anything."

"We are together now at last," he said, "and we are masters of our destiny. We are two matadors, and in our lives, each day will be a brand-new expedition where whatever we imagine, we will do! But we have had enough adventure for this day. We overcame a mountain!"

"Yes, we did, and you are fortunate that you are still alive," she scoffed. "You wanted passion? So you had me stranded on a mountain where I could have died! I had a knife. I could have killed you, after all!"

"I thought of that, but then you would have been alone," he laughed, "and it is still the early afternoon. The day ahead is long and glorious!" He raised a wineglass. "Let us drink to that!"

"Of course," she said and raised her own, "so let us drink to celebrate a long and glorious day!"

They tapped their glasses and they kissed. A moment later, while in thought, Antonio, he could not help but grin.

"But I remember earlier today. Still I can see the murderous expression on your face while on the mountain as we walked!" he teased, "when that cold rain began to fall, when pouring down so much on us! I looked into your eyes, and never have I seen such want to kill a man in any bull that I have ever fought!"

"Yes, I was angry, I admit" she smiled, "until you slipped and fell and tumbled down the slippery slope while bouncing, flailing all about and covered all with mud! I feared that you would not arise, but when you did, I could not stop from laughing at the spectacle. Then it was you who was outraged."

"I did not slip," he said, "since it was you who pushed me down. While I retrieved the contents of your ruined bag, you gave a kick to my behind to send me tumbling down!"

"That is not true," she giggled then. "Myself, I slipped and fell against you, bracing and allowing you to fall instead of me. I figured that you would not mind, as I remembered that I am the wife who you profess to love so much."

"And yet together we prevailed against the rainstorm and the mountain," he maintained. "And in this way our marriage will be strong and will endure. We had our heated moments and our challenges, but in the end, we reached the top embraced and walking step for step as one. In life together, we must not forget that we have faced adversity as one, and we have overcome."

"It is our second wedding night together," Isabella said. "Whatever will we do?"

"Let us return tonight to fair Madrid, where you were born," he answered her. "If I would be an understanding husband and your complement, we must begin first at Madrid."

"I am in Casablanca now, at *Mano de Dios*," Isabella challenged him. "And on tomorrow I will see the hand of God. If you, my husband, wish to travel to Madrid, then you should go there now, but I will stay at Casablanca in this castle here."

"And so will I, beside my wife," he said. "Though you will take me to Madrid tonight, but only through contrivance of your voice and memory. Tonight, I wish to lie with you and hold you close to me to listen to your voice."

"And that was all you wanted on your second wedding night, *Señor*?" I asked. "To *listen* to her voice?"

"A woman, first of all, is never what you see, Morisco," he returned, "since she is more of what you do *not* see. She is instead what she has lived, what she has felt. And always there is joy and sadness, happiness and pain. To understand a woman is to recognize what makes her feel in order to discover whether it is fear or loneliness or lack of love or anger, scorn or jealousy. Or she may feel the lack of being needed, heard or understood. And then there are the inward scars, some small and others more significant, some healed and others crusted over, raw or bleeding still. The conflicts and the memories within her mind and heart make up her very soul."

"A man can make a woman share those things?" I asked aloud. "Some personal, some painful—others deeply buried for the purpose of protection of her sanity?"

"He cannot *make* her share," he said. "But he can only help her feel secure and safe, non-judged and loved. Then he sincerely asks and listens to her voice. With time and patience, she will bare her heart and mind, and there will be a close connection after that, a bond for life."

"And Isabella? Did she share that night?" I asked.

"I held her as she started slowly, telling superficial things," he sighed, "and as she talked and understood that I was interested in all she said, she then began to share the closely guarded secrets of her heart, the puzzling concerns at first, and then the deeper things—of how her arm was broken by her father beating her, of how her one-time homeless family had to beg in shame, of being raped at age fourteen, this by a trusted teacher, and of being married off at age fifteen, this to an old and filthy uncle for one month of rent, of flight from him and education and redemption and a sense of self-respect not easily earned.

"Oh how she cried that night! And begged for peace, for end to her pathetic life, for love unearned and undeserved, for sympathy and worthiness. And as she wept, I wept, and as her heart was broken, so was mine."

I watched the melting of the maestro's face as tears streamed down, while I could not hold back my own.

"The horns were gone," he said, "*Muleta* gone, arena nowhere near, the steel, the shouts from crowds, the ceremony non-important there as we embraced—no matador, no bull. The only meaning was two hearts that pounded close together, full of love, ambition and the hope for happy life ahead. And after we could cry no more, we prayed. We begged for mercy and for blessing from the god of sun and shade. And lying there, we fell asleep and slept embracing, limbs enmeshed, until the morning light."

The maestro sipped the final drop of port left in his glass.

"I knew it from the moment that we touched," he sighed, "That night was magic, on our second wedding night.

"When we awoke the next auspicious day, the both of us, we knew that ours would be a life of wondrous adventure with no rules, except to love each other in this life and in whatever lies beyond."
He smiled, remembering the day.

"The sun was shining in the sky *azul!*" he said. "We had an early breakfast and we made an escapade back down the mountainside, recovering the treasures we had lost from broken bags in pouring rain the day before. Most of the things, we found, but our enjoyment was in our adventure as we went. We had a simple lunch along the beach that day and splashed around like children, playing in the foam-capped waves. We wrote our secret wishes in the sand, and as the sun was falling toward the sea, we went back up the mountain to the villa there."

"It was your final wedding day?" I asked. "And were you able on that day to watch the sunset from the balcony?"

"It was magnificent, Morisco," Maestro nodded as he smiled, "To stand alone with her, before the shining sun, to watch it plunge into the swirling sea from such a lofty place! In all my life, I never saw such brightness and such glory as we did that day! And humbled, we removed our shoes. I had the hand of Isabella in my own as quietly we turned our trembling bodies toward each other, faces close. And from the corners of our outward squinting eyes, the both of us, we saw the *hand of God!* Yes, it was clearly there, but when we quickly turned in reasonable astonishment, it simply was not there to see with naked human eyes.

"We stood in silence, mute, as words were inappropriate. Yet we had seen the hand of God, and from that day the hand of God was in our lives. We felt it, guiding us, accomplishing what was impossible, inspiring us. And in that very moment, lovely Isabella Zamora Castañeda and Antonio Castañeda de Castilla were then joined as man and wife. It was a glorious day!"

"But you had ceased to be Antonio!" I countered then. "You were Fernando at that time!"

"Two marriages," he answered me. "The first before all men, the other before God, who long ago had written secret marriage vows on both our hearts. As we looked toward the setting sun that day, within that very moment we were married before God, but not until that time. You sigh and seem to disbelieve, Morisco. Does my story not make sense to you?"

"I do not know. The hand of God!" I laughed. "I do not have your faith. If even I believed there *was* a god, then I imagine he would be invisible to us. No one could see the hand of God!"

"But it is everywhere!" he sighed. "You see it with your heart, but only if your heart has learned to understand that sight is more than what you see. My Isabella, she and I, we had a splendid life of love and wealth and travel and adventure! Yes, we felt the earthquake of the wildebeest in Tanzania and the heated jungle breath in hidden forests all along the *Marañón*. We drank peyote potions with Comanche holy men in ancient ceremonies and we spent three weeks consuming whales and seals with Eskimos, while getting fat. We took a pilgrimage to Santiago and a second one to Rome and still a third to what they call the Holy Land. We danced with *Zulus* and we learned the *Kuchipudi* steps in India.

"We went to castles, dined with princes and with kings and presidents. We had a dinner with the Roman Pontiff at our home, this very house! We waded into rivers: Nile, Zambezi, Mississippi, Volga, Yangtze and the Amazon. We traveled to the ends of Earth. We ate all things that could be eaten and we drank perhaps one thousand casks of wine. We climbed to highest mountaintops and dove from there into the hidden caverns of the deepest seas. We gave imagination life and we gave passion to the ordinary days we lived! Yet everywhere we went, if we were still and contemplative, we would see the hand of God that led our lives."

"Oh, what a privileged life that you have lived, *Señor*," I said. "If I could live a life like yours, perhaps I too would see the hand of God!"

"Unshut your eyes, Morisco!" Maestro urged me then. "You see things in reverse. It is the hand of God that makes a life of wonder, passion and adventure possible, but first you must *believe*."

"Perhaps," I sighed. "It was your final wedding night, and you were at the villa only for three days. The first night, as you said, you had 'explored' her flesh, and on the second night you discovered what was in her mind. And what did you uncover on the third?"

"The third night was sublime, perfection realized," he smiled. "Again, for her I ran a bath, with flowers, spices, wine and candles, music playing softly in the room. This time, I slipped into the tub behind and wrapped myself around, from back to front. The water was so soft and warm, and dripping from the *lufah* sponge I used to gently scrub and stimulate her back and neck. I drizzled water through her hair in order to massage her scalp, her brow, her cheeks, her chin. I trailed a stream of water over tingling, rising breasts and all across her shoulders and her nape. I kissed that special place behind her neck, and then I rose and left the copper tub.

'Now come to bed and let me pleasure you,' I said. "And when she came, I kissed her then one hundred times in random places, counting each aloud to build anticipation. Only then the flower, full of nectar, glistening with dew—it bloomed before my eyes."

Luis returned to check the fireplace and to remove our empty glasses. Then he offered to dispense the cognac, but the maestro told him to return in thirty minutes time, and then he turned toward me.

"In your own life, Morisco, have you ever really looked upon a flower when in bloom?" he asked.

"Of course, I have, Señor," I answered quickly, not perceiving what he meant.

"I am referring to the flower of a woman," he continued then. "If you have never made the time to stop to take a close examination of this flower with your eyes and with your senses, you cannot appreciate its nature and the beauty of the bloom."

"You understood it even in your youth, Señor? You understood the nature and the beauty of that flower even then?" I asked.

"This flower is the absolute most vulnerable, most powerful, most splendid feature of a woman, melding heart and mind," he said, "and yet it properly should be a private offering. If she is indiscriminate, then it gives off a stench. Yet if it blooms for love, it will effuse the most delightful and provocative bouquet. This flower, soft and delicate, alluring—is the source of her attraction, which transcends the sexual, platonic and the spiritual. Yet if the man or woman does not pay attention so to nurture to the flower's needs, then it will never bloom, or if it opens, it will quickly wilt."

"What does this flower need?" I asked.

"Those needs involve consideration of the smallest detail," he responded then, "to know the flower and its intimate design, the phases and the hues, the outline and anatomy, the individual reaction—no two flowers truly are the same—and also paying keen attention to the soft and luscious petals and the shy reactive stigma in its hiding place, and most important then, the sweet and sticky nectary.

"It means alighting and attending with the grace and softness of a butterfly, the diligence and purpose of a honeybee, the intellect and singular responsiveness of an exclusive hummingbird. As such I visited the flower blossoming through Isabella on that night and was rewarded with ambrosia, the finest nectar in the natural world. I lingered, hovered there perhaps one hour, then I rediscovered all the secret pleasure places I had found two nights before.

"There is a time when every dance must end, at last a time when the opponent is subdued, for only then the orchid opens wide and readies to receive, when sweet surrender comes. And at that moment is a merging of the opposites: the hard and soft, the in and out, the strong and gentle, savage-tame, the predator and prey, the hunger-gluttony, the power-weakness, the abandon and restraint, control and vulnerability.

"So after waiting for so many years, Isabella finally was mine. She was my wife, and she was in my bed, with petals full of color and engorged. She finally was ready to receive her fleshly portion due from me."

He closed his eyes a moment, savoring, remembering.

"At last, the slow and sensual merging of two bodies, rigid sword into the soft and lubricated sheath—then sliding slowly and unhurriedly, right to the hilt. And next the steady, gentle and deliberate introduction which, in pleasured time, gave way to more aggressive exposition and a quickening of pace, and all within a theme created by the animating music as it played. Exhilaration sped the tempo, well beyond *crescendo*, *pianoforte*, bold and passionate, and with increased exhilaration while the cymbals crashed, and drumrolls boomed to sighs in harmony.

A pause for catching breath, and then a second movement in another key, and with a cadence faster still, a sensual sonata at the edge of ecstasy. And then a third and fourth and fifth in quick succession. By that time, our bodies fused, eventually becoming one in rhythm and intensity. Our spirits merged so we could not distinguish where I ended or where she began. And then a sixth and seventh time! That night, Morisco—on that night was not a consummation of our marriage as you are inclined to think. It was through God a consummation of our love... a consummation of our hearts."

He closed his fist and tapped his chest three times while choking up. His voice was strained and guttural. "*¡Los corazones!*"

Tercio de Muerte

Luis, the steward, came into the room, and he, with keen attention and with careful ceremony, poured the Remy Martin *Louis XIII* into elaborate crystal cognac glasses, filled half-full, all three of them.

"What is the hour now, Morisco?" stretching, Maestro asked.

"One hour past the middle of the night," I yawned, though unintentionally, "but please continue with the story you are telling me."

I squinted, looking back toward the door through which Luis had left and then I looked upon the glasses on the tabletop.

"Luis is going to drink this one with us?" I asked. "He poured three glasses, then he left?"

"Three glasses," Maestro smiled while taking up the goblet nearest him. "This one for me, and one for you, and then the third is for the angel who has come today."

"The angel?" I half-laughed. "*What* angel comes today?"

"The Angel, 'Death,'" Señor insisted as he pushed the glass before an empty space. "I always pour an extra portion for the angel at my table every time I plan to go into the ring. It comes as no surprise that when you are a matador, you spend much time within the company of this angelic guardian. If you are fortunate, then maybe you will get to know his mien. And yet if you are truly special, he might show you great compassion by extending mercy in that fated hour when he comes at last to gently guide you on the journey home."

"The Grim Reaper?" I asked. "You pour an extra glass of cognac for a fantasy—the Grim Reaper then?"

"Grim Reaper! ¡Pah, cabrón!" he groaned, disgusted then. "A fiction for the infidels. This fantasy is nothing but a foolish panacea for the uninformed! The *angel* is from God, and so his mission is benign and merciful. It is a grim assignment, yes, and so his aspect must be grave. There is no 'reaping' of the souls, or lives, the way the ignorant believe. The angel takes a place among us meant to lead and comfort us from this dominion to the next."

"But you believe that you have *seen* this angel?" I inquired. "What is his appearance in your estimation?"

"Oh, he is very tall at times, but not at all the times," he answered me. "His flowing robe is one belonging to the sons of God, though it is dark. His wings are black, which he keeps folded at his back. But when he spreads them out, their span is quite enormous, inspiring awe. His face is but a fleshless skull—without expression, without age, without a tongue to speak a single word, and yet his presence brings great peace to those who see him and as well to those who do not have the mind to see."

"And does he drink the cognac that you pour for him?" I wondered then, aloud.

"The cognac is a *brindis* off'ring that I pour to honor him," *Señor* explained. "In my own mind, I think he sips the spirit from the liquid part, but my imagining might be my overworked imagination. Always—on every night before I fight a match, before the sun, I pour it out, upon the ground for him."

"And does this angel have a name?" I asked.

"The name is not important," he returned. "The angel does not seek to have us call his name, but he exists to comfort us. Yet there are some who call him *Michael*—(*Gabriel* for kings), while others call to *Azrael* or *Sammael* or *Mairya* too and other names, but what we call him does not matter much. To merely call his name is vain, though he will find the ones who suffer and will always be there when the time has come for him to comfort them. I saw him on the day Fernando died."

Señor imbibed again the aromatic blend of concentrated wines.

"Your look is one of mocking, though I know you do not mean to mock me in my home. I understand that you do not believe there is an angel over death. Am I not right, Morisco?" he proposed.

"Not truly," I admitted with a shrug. "I am a man of practicality, and so I find it difficult believing in such things."

"Do you believe that unseen beings can exist—true beings lacking carnal form, who thus cannot be seen with eyes?" he asked. "Do you believe there is a spirit counterpart to all things physical?"

"No, I do not believe," I answered him. "But neither do I disbelieve, so I am not convinced. You see this angel in your mind?"

"Not *in* my mind," he said, "but *with* my mind, which is the spirit part of who I am. And with a spiritual perspective, anyone may see and understand the spiritual things that God has meant for us to see and understand."

"And how does one acquire this spiritual vision you describe?" I asked. "Moreover, how does one discover how to see things with the mind? Can this be taught?"

"Oh, what a needless question!" Maestro laughed aloud. "You cannot learn a thing that you already know! How does one gain this vision of the mind? The answer is not complicated. You must simply shut your eyes to open them."

Amazement overwhelming me, I sipped the ancient *eau de vie* within the glass. So viscous, though so smooth! The cognac lingered in my tightened throat. I closed my eyes and searched, but I saw nothing there, and then I looked back toward the maestro where he sat.

"And when you were at last the married counterpart to Isabella—when she was your wife" I redirected then, "did you continue on to fight the bulls on plaza sands?"

"Of course, I did!" he said. "I fought for one more year in Spain and Mexico, in France and Argentina. So it was that everywhere I went, the sun was always in the sky to shine on me. My wife was always there."

He stopped, as if to suddenly remember something lost.

"And then I fought the bull, called *el Pesar*. This bull, Morisco, please remember this—this bull was unlike any other bull that I had ever fought. ¡*Enigma*! ¡*Catedral*! A huge, unnatural *whitish* bull with overlarge and narrow horns, set forward under fiery, reddish eyes. And he was from a line of blood that sought revenge on me and family. In irony, in *brindis* ceremony, I conceived to dedicate this bull, *Pesar*—to dedicate him to the memory of my fallen brother who the world had called Antonio, and to his soul which was, of course, *my* guilty soul.

"The bull, he came out quickly, standing there before me," then *Señor* explained, "*Pesar* was neither moving, neither being then inclined to move. As such, I looked into his eyes, which lacking color, lacked the necessary screens or barriers that separated man and beast, and Hell from Earth. Until that moment, I never had imagined that perhaps a bull could have a soul, and so perhaps this bull did not.

"I swear to you, Morisco, on that day, I did believe I *saw* a soul in him, and worse, the soul of my departed brother called Fernando. This is true. I saw his soul within the reddish, glowing eyes of one white-colored, supernatural bull. And so while you may think that I am separated from my own good sense, I still believe I saw the essence of my brother there within its eyes."

"And did you fight this bull?" I asked.

"Well naturally, Morisco, I was startled by this bull," he said. "To think that I had looked upon the spirit of Fernando in its eyes! And I remembered then that I had twice betrayed my oath to him, as I swore never to reveal what we had done that day we traded places many years before. I swore it on his soul and on the soul of my departed father even as my brother died. I promised not to share our secret, not unless within the presence of the angel, with exception on the day that I would die.

"But twice I had betrayed that oath. At first when I at last admitted to Veronica that I was not Fernando who she loved, on that same day when she in anger tried to stab my heart. And then to Isabella—I revealed to her the details of that secret on our second wedding night. The passing of a dozen years had weakened me to rationalize that it no longer mattered after so much time. A broken vow, a brother and a father thus betrayed. I could not help but thinking that this bull was sent to punish me, to mete out justice for my promise unfulfilled.

"I dropped my guard, preparing to be gored and savaged by this bull, but then I saw the face of Isabella in the crowd, and only then I realized that she would never watch me die, that destiny would take her first. The bull was strong and smart and stout of heart, but Fate was on my side. And every time it seemed the bull would have advantage over me, the angel intervened. And finally, the bull grew slow and heavy with fatigue. With great reluctance, I exchanged the wooden imitation for a sword of steel in preparation for the kill.

"Defeated, disappointed and disheartened, *el Pesar*, he looked at me, into my eyes, and only then I was convinced for certain that the heavens had a part in this! And with the spirit of Fernando set in opposition, then I understood the judgment meant for me. Cruel destiny ordained that I would have to stab my brother through his heart in order to appreciate the graveness of my broken oath. I raised my eyes with hope, appealing to the acting *Presidente* and the crowd. I wished that he or they would move to spare the life of such a valiant bull, but no such mercy came. The stadium was silent for a moment as my gaze returned to *el Pesar* while standing, wobbling there, with eyes that seemed to be Fernando's eyes.

"I hesitated there at first, and then I lunged as I had lunged perhaps two thousand times before. *¡Ay Perpendicular! ¡Ay Dios mío, el Pesar!*—the bull leaned forward in the instant that I drove the sword, and so I missed his heart. The *estocada* then was through his *lung* and seemed to cause the bull great pain! He stumbled to his knees, unbreathing, coughing, bleeding from his mouth and from his nose. I missed the heart! So in the end, I did not know the place Fernando's true heart lied."

"For all to see, his bright red blood was dripping as he tried to rise and fell onto his side, legs stiffening with spasms as he struggled there. *Pesar* was gasping, drowning in the blood that bubbled from his nostrils—he was fighting hard to fill his lungs. At once the crowd could see that I had failed to pierce the heart. The *pitos* came, the whistles from the crowd, and then the *bronca*, showing how they disapproved that I had missed the mark.

"And contrary to what some misinformed Americans believe, the crowds of Andalucía and all of Spain," he said, "will not endure for very long to see a bull in pain and suffering. *El presidente* stood, concerned, and urged an end at once, immediate and clean. And so I took a second sword, called *verdugo*, and I performed the *descabello*, severing the spinal cord to free the bull from misery and life. And when at last *Pesar* was dying there, he heaved a heavy breath aloud that seemed to call my name. The sound was strange and eerily familiar. On that day, as even now, I swore that I was hearing my own brother's voice. Fernando called my name! He did, Morisco, on that day!"

"I was so moved and filled with guilt," he said, "that I at once took up the sword in order for *cortar la coleta*. With that sword, I cut the braided pigtail that I wore behind my neck. In doing this before the crowd, it was a signal that I was retired from the ring, and I have never fought another bull until this day."

"So many things, *Señor!*" reluctantly I spoke. "So much bizarre coincidence and circumstance! The hand of God in Casablanca and the bloodline of these bulls, this angel that you see who drinks with you at night, and now there's more? Your brother was this *bull*? Please help me understand!"

"Ah, there is nothing strange, Morisco," then he laughed. "When you are looking back on over eighty-seven years of life, and you have lived them to the full, you too will be as difficult to understand. For this much I have learned: when we are young, we are completely physical—our needs, desires and ambitions, our perception of the world around us. But this changes as we live and grow, if we are fortunate enough and wise to live to some great age. For over time will come the slow progression from our bodies to our minds, from fleshly ignorance to spiritual understanding in its stead."

The maestro motioned toward the raging fire in the hearth, where, struggling, Luis was putting on another log.

"The wood in there begins as physical in all respects," he said, "but life, which is the fire, will transform a thing once physical to something having spiritual qualities, and all that will remain will be a cast, the ashen residue, which blows away. It is a process natural in many things. Though in the end, 'where is the wood?' In burning, it transformed from physical to spiritual, while it provided light and warmth, which is the legacy of burning wood. For now, I must remain within this frail and insubstantial cast and give off light to you, but soon my spirit will be free of it.

"If you are fortunate, Morisco, if you pray for understanding as I did, perhaps you will be granted sight to see the spiritual things in your experience. But you are right. Not everyone will have this sight. It is a blessing to be sure, but must be sought, developed, ever valued as a precious gift."

He bowed his head, regretting and remembering.

"My son José, he was the opposite extreme," he sighed. "Not only did he disbelieve, he actually disdained all spiritual things. To him, there was no god, no good, no higher purpose or inequity or sin, and no consideration for redemption in his heart or mind. From early on, I saw that he was purely physical, the same as all the bulls he fought—aggressive, savage and with blood so hot that it would often rob his brain of common sense.

"My son was passion without thought and power without discipline, intelligence without pragmatic reasoning. I tried to talk to him, to help him to consider that the flame of life in every man will gradually transform him from the physical to spiritual. I told him that the man who does not understand this change will live a shortened life, an ignorant existence, right until the moment that he dies."

The stubborn log that burned within the hearth popped loudly, hissing for a while, releasing steam from some internal cavity, still green and moist. Luis came in and poked the log, and seconds later, it became engulfed in bright orange streaming violent flames, and seemed to roar in protest to the intervention.

"Though by this time, your Josélito was a man," I then surmised. "And did he, over time, become a capable bullfighter in the manner that he wanted since he was a boy? Was he a maestro like his father was? Or like his 'uncle' was?"

"When I retired," Maestro said, "it seemed that every bullfighter from Spain to Argentina came—with some to praise and others who would denigrate the name of Castañeda de Castilla, though they coveted the legacy that I relinquished in the ring. They came for an inheritance—my mantle as the best torero fighting bulls, the favorite matador of all the world."

He motioned toward a portrait of a proud young man who wore a splendid, gold and midnight blue *traje de luces*—right hand upon his hip, his left hand on the hilt of sword and head held back in arrogance. His *montera* was tilted to one side atop his head. The model of a matador, and yet he seemed to be a boy in clothing of a man.

"José was younger than them all," the maestro said. "He had eighteen or nineteen years of age, when they had, many of that lot, the equal to his age the years of fighting bulls. While some were good, and some well-celebrated, José, my son, possessed unusual intensity. And when the bulls came out, José went to the fight with such ferocity that many of the bravest bulls, on sensing his impassioned blood, would cower toward the shade, avoiding him. And always, in the end—the clean and the decisive kill, and so José became a favorite of the crowds.

"To be a matador is for a man to live and breathe a passionate life," *Señor* continued as he closed his eyes. "To risk a sudden, painful death in the arena rather than to live a long and pitiful existence, save adventure, and without the thrill of ever doing something that we know a very few on Earth can do. To die with heated blood, a racing, pounding heart, a lust fulfilled, to master destiny instead of growing old in mediocrity, while never tasting glory, clinging to an insubstantial life until the time the angel comes to pry our fingers from unvarnished posts, to die in bed! *¡Ay, Dios mío!* There is no other life worth living, my last heir, except to be a matador."

Confused at once, then I began to speak, but he had not concluded yet.

"There is no other death worth dying, none except to die upon the plaza sand." He wiped his eyes while silent weeping with a silk embroidered handkerchief and looked toward me.

"It took six months to pass before José became the favorite matador in all the world," he said. "The other matadors were very good, no doubt, while never taking chances, where secretly they would instruct their teams to punish bulls beyond the customary practices to make the fight unfair, so that the overwhelming odds were with the matador, and by this means avoiding danger in the ring.

"José was young, and as it was with me, he had no fear. He took on risks and chances that no other matador would dare. He put himself in jeopardy with powerful and dangerous bulls, so that his victories were impressive and spectacular. I merely danced with bulls, but he would seem to hug them tight. He held them close, and for this cause and other reasons he was called *el Amante*, which means of course, 'the lover,' which was true for bulls and women too: he held them close and pierced their hearts."

"And was your son a better matador than you?" I asked.

"How can I say?" he answered. "His approach to life and mine were very different. But if I knew one thousand women in my time, my son José had in his bed ten thousand girls, and never loved a single one, and neither did he care. For after every victory, the girls would come, and he would have his way with every one of them, the large and small, the beautiful and foul, the wise and simple-minded girls from Spain to Ecuador, and to the Orient and Africa. Like Solomon, his many paramours beyond his wives would be impossible to count, so I am certain that I have at least one hundred *nietos* scattered all about."

"So many to descend from you!" incredulously I asked. "And did you know a single one of them?"

"Well no, Morisco" *Señor* breathed, "and I do not believe that even José did. But does a bull take time to know his children's names? And will a beast take care to know what will become of them? José embraced the physical, the blood and lust, and he rejected everything he could not see, and so his children were not real to him. He did not know, nor did he care."

"Then he seems hardly your own son, *Señor*" I said. "I think of him in that same way Fernando thought of you. What made him different from the bulls he fought? Was he a man who fought with bulls? Was he a beast and who when, within the ring, was quarreling with another beast?"

"What elevates a man," he answered, "is capacity for transformation from the physical to spiritual. And you are right! When I was young, I thought and acted in the way that my José behaved. But as the fire burned, that transformation turned the fleshly beast into a spiritual man. It is the flame of life that changes us. And yet, José—it seemed that he would not be changed."

"What do you mean?" I asked.

"Well, I debated him at length for many times," he said, "but he disdained and only ridiculed the things I said. I told him that the transformation was a natural process in the life of every man—that he should let the fire burn, but he would not. He tried to snuff it out instead. And then he turned on me."

"And why should I place value in your words, the abject *failure* that you are!" José shot back. "For all the reputation that my grandfather and uncle earned, you shamed our family name—you first avoided destiny and finally you walked away from glory totally humiliated and disgraced: an overestimated matador, so clueless that you did not realize you lost your edge. Your name is an embarrassment to all our family. You should have died out there! You killed that bull, the one called *el Pesar*, but he defeated you as well, discrediting your reputation, causing you alone to put at risk the honored legacy of Castañeda de Castilla for all time."

"My name will live beyond that fated, feted match," *Señor* responded then, "and memory of me beyond this life. And when the book is closed, then I will be remembered for my willingness to grow and learn and feel compassion. Then my flame will warm, inspire and will stir a multitude of minds to trust enough to gaze beyond the physical, to gain enlightenment. If you continue as a beast, José, then you will *die* a beast, and not a man—your life and history unworthy of remembrance or praise."

"What good does memory, Papa, when you are *dead*?" José replied. "I do not care to be remembered by the fools and many cuckold men who watch but do not live. They are unworthy of my second thoughts. I live exclusively to revel in the daily thrill of killing bulls and celebrating with the women in the night. My life is here and now. I do not care to have it written in a book. When I am dead, the universe will end for me. There is no more."

"This life is but the shadow of a greater plan," *Señor* continued. "For the spiritual man, a *cast* is left behind, and life continues in the memory of God. But for the man who is not spiritual, the cast is merely dust that blows away into the wind, and nothing lives beyond. This man has lived a life of vanity."

"And what of my 'forgotten' uncle, your departed twin?" José returned, "and what of brave Antonio Castañeda de Castilla who, by all accounts, remains the greatest bullfighter who ever lived? What would you say of him, Papa? He was never spiritual like you, as he was physical in all his thinking and his ways.? I am like him the same. So did my uncle die a man, or did he perish as a beast? Was his a life of vanity?"

"That candid question from José," the maestro said to me as I continued taking notes. "That was a moment very difficult. For many years, I wished to tell José the truth, the truth that I had fathered him and was indeed Antonio, the celebrated matador of Spain. But such a thing would mean that I would have to tell him how he came to be conceived in lust instead of matrimony, of how his mother spent a week with me in bed within the month before she married my own brother. *¡Ay-yi-yi!*

"Then I would have to tell him that the man he had for years resented as a father was in fact his uncle—and the man who he admired and respected as his uncle was instead by blood his father. I would have to tell him that he was the first and only son belonging to Antonio Castañeda de Castilla. I could never tell him that!"

"I understand!" I said. "But you could not stop there."

"No!" he agreed. "Then I would have to tell him of the day that changed the lives for both of us, Fernando's life and mine, of how we argued over what was best, to be a matador in flesh, or be a matador in life, of how we traded places for a single day. And on that afternoon, it was Fernando on the sand, instead of me, who fought *Muerte* to the death. It was Fernando, on that day, who fought the greatest bullfight of all time, and finally, it was Fernando, tempting Fate, who died in the arena on the day of April third and swore me to a mocking oath.

"But all of this I never told José or any other soul," he said, "and so in answer to that candid question from José: he asked me if Antonio, his 'uncle,' lived a life of vanity. I answered, 'he did not, although he died a death of vanity.'"

"If only I could die so vainly in the ring," José maintained, "as I live only for the thought that I one day will die out there, but only after having fought the perfect match, and with the world who watched in awe. How is that vanity, or beastly reasoning? Still I recall the celebration of my uncle's life on television—how he died while perched upon the pinnacle of Nebo, looking out—all on his greatest day! Although you call it vain, his death inspired me. And what is the alternative? To live so long to be imprisoned by the frailty of age, this 'so-called' fire barely flickering and burning cold? To die in bed? There is no profit there. There is no *passion* there! From Fate I beg a short and glorious life! For in the end, the desperate lives of mice and men are vanity."

"On hearing these well-spoken words," *Señor* said thoughtfully, "I realized that even though my son was outwardly opposed and unaware, the fire was transforming him. I ceased that day to fret about my son, José."

"Was his career a long one?" I inquired.

"Oh, he fought many bulls, and won in glorious form," the maestro said, "because he did not fear to die. He welcomed death, invited tragedy. He turned his back on charging bulls and stepped aside precisely when it seemed that he would be annihilated by the angry animal. He took outrageous jeopardies and chances all for glory sake. And always at the end, a risky move, a thrill, excitement right until the final stroke, which always was spectacular, inspiring sighs and moans and great applause! In all of Andalucían memory, there never was a more exciting matador! However, Fate, the poet-weaver, answered in three years his prayer to have a short and glorious life!"

"Three years, *Señor*?" I questioned him. "What happened to your son?"

"There was one fiery bull," he said, "whose name among the matadors was *Némesis*, and who was not the strongest or the smartest bull José had ever faced, and yet it seemed he was created for the moment that he faced my son. I warned José before the match. I warned him of the bull that he would have to face, and of the bloodline threat. From when my father fought the bulls in fields, this bloodline stalked our family. It maimed my father, and it killed my brother right before my eyes. *Diablo* came from there!

"And from the start this bull would do the opposite of what José expected him to do. When led toward left, he broke toward right, when stirred to anger, he continued to stay calm, when moved to charge, he held his place. He seemed to know well in advance the very thinking of José.

"Now this confused my son, so his bravado and his well-known poise and style were never evident all while he struggled with this bull. As minutes slowly passed, it was a grueling match. José relied on all the lessons he had learned and fought his greatest fight. *Arrimarse!*—that is what the crowd began to chant. And then the bull, he fought with such intensity so that it seemed his heart would burst.

"The day was overcast with gloom. A shadow came. Dark, gray-black clouds, it seemed, were hanging just above the stands. The wind blew intermittently and cold and caused an eerie chill throughout the crowd. I see it now—while seated in the *delanteras*, in the front, I easily was close enough to see the frantic eyes and face belonging to my handsome son and then the black, implacable expression of the vengeful bull.

"There was a point at which José began to realize the poet, Fate, had intervened, that destiny had chosen him to die on that dark afternoon. And in one moment unexpected as he paused, I sensed a change in him. It might be my imagining, but I believe I saw his transformation in one single breath.

"José had struggled to complete a difficult, impressive pass, and as he, still off-balance, struggled to correct his form, the bull, then turning quick around, began at once toward him. José, instead of quick preparing for the charge to step aside, he looked up toward the sky and seemed to nod toward me, an offer of acceptance—and he then faced his life."

"But do you mean his death?" I asked. "José was gored by *Némesis*? Was this his end?"

"It was a glorious end. He boldly stood to face this charging bull that pierced his torso with a horn and tossed him thirty feet into the center on the plaza sand. And oddly, *Némesis* did not attack again. His destiny fulfilled, he trotted off into the shade, where he collapsed and died.

"Your only son!" I interrupted then. "And did he die that day?"

"I hurried to the place beneath the plaza, *la enfermería*, where they took him on a board," the maestro said, a salty fluid, overwhelming saddened eyes. "The wound was mortal to his vital organs, physical and spiritual. The sheets were twisted on the bed and soaked with purple blood and agony. And yet José had found a place of calm within his mind. He smiled to welcome me."

"A short and glorious life!" he groaned aloud. "And at the end, it all makes sense to me!"

"I looked beside the bed," the old man said. "Across from me and in a corner, I could see the angel standing there, his mien as always, grim and serious. And when I looked upon the faces of the doctors who attended my José, the heavenly appointment of the angel was confirmed. I knew José would die."

Señor recalled that even as he gazed upon his dying son, the crowds above were chanting still the name José Antonio Castañeda de Castilla, thinking that his son would live. It broke his heart, he said, to see the end of his own flesh that day. And with the angel looking on, he finally resolved that he would share the secret with his son.

"José, please listen now and know I am your father," broken-heartedly he said, "but know I am *Antonio* Castañeda de Castilla in reality. It's true! Fernando was my *brother*, my identical, and yet my opposite. The both of us, we loved your mother, Isabella, very much. And quarrelling, my brother challenged me to take his place before his classes while he took my place upon the plaza sand, but only for one day. We meant no harm to anyone.

"And on that crucial day, in one chaotic afternoon did Fate play an ironic trick on us. Fernando fought the greatest fight in history and died in place of me, while I was forced to live in secret the remainder of his life. You are my son, the only son belonging to Antonio Castañeda de Castilla, one in all the world!"

"Papa," he strained, "In further irony, your secret was already known to me before today. Two nights ago, my mother told me everything, the story of her life and yours. And hearing it, I longed to be a better man, to understand what higher passion is, to be like you, a matador!"

"You are a matador, José," the maestro said. "The very *best!*"

"In the arena, yes," José affirmed in agony while struggling to breathe. "In the arena I am called a matador, when I am nothing more than a performer on the sand, perhaps a matador in death."

José reached out a bloody hand to touch his father's tear-drenched face.

"But *you* are, more than all, a matador within your *heart*, Papa, a matador in life!"

He coughed a bloody mouthful and continued, wheezing as he spoke.

"You are the man I long to be... if only as I die," he wept. "And I am proud to live and die your son, the only son belonging to Antonio Castañeda de Castilla... Please! Please tell the people who I am! I have not died a beast..."

"José, he looked toward a darkened place beside the bed and shuddered as he fixed his eyes," the old man said.

"¡El ángel!" my son exclaimed, "I see the angel standing there! I see him with my heart and mind!" and smiling, gazing at that seeming empty space, José expired, open eyes."

The maestro wept a moment for his son, who died so long ago, and then he sipped the cognac from the glass, and raising it, he motioned toward my own.

"Please drink with me," he said. "¡Al ángel de Dios! And to my fallen son, José!"

I followed, raising my own glass, admiring his confidence, "We drink to faith! And to José."

Again, we had to take a fifteen-minute break because the maestro had to serve a summons of his bladder in the lavatory down the hall. When he returned, I tried to redirect discussion toward a lighter subject. Nonetheless, eventually I realized Señor had planned this night for many years. He closed his eyes and took a breath, remembering the place he left, and then resumed.

"You probably are wondering why," he said, "that after I was finally united with my wife, with Isabella—why the two of us, we had no other children born."

"I wondered that," I said.

"We tried," he sad admitted, "and we never knew the cause or reasoning. We did not know in who or where fault could lie—in me or her or in the sky. Although we prayed for children as an added joy, the flower of her womb would wilt each month and would produce no fruit. But there are things we must accept in life, while never knowing why. And so we did and we enjoyed instead the benefits of less responsibility.

"An empty nest, we flew to places we had never dreamt to go before, to Borneo and Nepal, to Zimbabwe and Belize and Trinidad, to the Galapagos, Jerusalem and Lebanon. And all where we imagined, we would go. And when we went, we ate the food and drank the drink. We ate the soil and we swilled the sea. *Dios mío!* We had the most extraordinary life!"

He bowed his head and quietly began to weep.

"And then my Isabella, ah, my wife," he sighed and wagged his head. "My wife! My wife! She fell to illness, and the doctors did not give her very long to live—less than one year. It was a cancer that had stolen lives from many women in the world, a cancer of the cervical. Can you imagine that? To love someone so long to have a doctor tell you that your story would be over in one year! Of course, at first we both were angry and at once denied belief. But then the symptoms showed in her, the loss of weight and appetite and then her tiredness. When after seven months had passed, we knew the end would come, and so we brought her niece to live with us, to comfort her until the angel came.

"I asked her if there was a thing we had not done in all our years," he said, "a journey we had failed to undertake. I told her that it did not matter where, but we would go. She answered that, in honor of her grandfather, her ﺟﺪ, who was a Moor, she wished to set upon a final pilgrimage to Mecca in Arabia."

"The pilgrimage? *The Hajj*?" I blurted out, remembering *my* ancestry. "It is a sacred duty of the Muslim faith, and not for undertaking by an infidel, if even for a natural curiosity."

"I said the same," he said, "but she insisted it was ritual that dated back to *Ibrahim*, or Abraham, and therefore sacred to a greater faith. The 'son of old,' Ezekiel, he made this pilgrimage, she said. For all her life she wished to undertake the journey," he continued, and "so how could I deny her last request?

"Of course, I made excuse," he said, "I told her that I was concerned about her health and that the pilgrimage would cause unnecessary risk and posed a threat to shorten her abbreviated life. And yet, as always, Isabella had her way.

"It was November, I remember. And in the month before, we drank no wine or took intoxicating drink. We prayed together every morning and at night, and on the day we left, she gave me clothes to wear, and leather sandals for my feet. She wore a simple smock with sandals of her own. Her hair was in a single braid, her face was plain and gaunt.

"From Tarifa in Cádiz, we took a ferry to Tangier and there we joined a camel caravan with other pilgrims who were headed to the harbor at Algiers. We took a boat from there across the

Mediterráneo and we met with several other thousand pilgrims who arrived at Port Said in Egypt's north. From there we took a train to Cairo, where we had arrived too late to catch our flight. One day behind our scheduled plan, we booked an evening flight to Jedda in Arabia and took up lodging there.

"And with each day that passed, I had to watch my Isabella growing weaker. I could see it in her eyes, and though she tried her best to be the optimist, I knew the heavy bleeding had returned," he said. "Oh, she was deathly tired every morning, even worse at night! Medina was not far away, but she was very ill. I found an Arab doctor who was known to treat successfully such illnesses, but she was at a loss for what to do."

"In all my practice, I have never seen a woman bleed so much and live," she said to me. "So if you love your wife, then you should take her back to Spain to let her die at home in peace."

"But Isabella was not hearing it," he sighed, remembering. "She came to see Medina and she wanted to see Mecca in Arabia."

"But you are not of Muslim faith," the doctor said, "and thus you are forbidden in the central city of Medina at this time, and you are not allowed at all in Mecca anywhere. This pilgrimage is not for you. Go home and find your peace with your *Romani* god in Spain."

"I made a promise to my grandfather, who was a Moor," my ailing wife returned. "He made the pilgrimage for seven times and was a son of Islam all his life. I promised him that I would one day make a pilgrimage to Mecca and Medina, if even I could not go in. He told me that the one true god, *Allah*, was god of every man, no matter what he called himself. And too my grandmother, his wife, who was a Jew for all her life, she said a prophet called *Habacuc* said that *Yahweh* was the one true god and was the god of every man. So if there is one god, then he does not forbid a single soul to honor him, which I have struggled, weak and suffering many miles to do. If any are offended or aggrieved because I came this far to look upon two holy cities, then they do not know God, no matter what they call themselves.

"God does not know religion or division or tradition even," Isabella said, "He only recognizes those who truly seek him with sincerity, with all the heart and mind. These are the true believers who are blessed to see beyond the mosque and church and synagogue. And all the rest—they all believe in leaders, blood and government, but they do not believe in God."

"And strangely, in that night," the maestro said, "We saw the hand of God again. The bleeding stopped and Isabella seemed to be restored with vital energy. We took a bus and traveled to Medina. All the while we spoke with pilgrims from the many places we had visited. We shared the story of our journey and our faith as they did theirs. We found believers all along the way, this pilgrimage. In doing so, we learned to understand that in the life of humankind, the journey is the most important thing. The journey teaches us, and it is where we live our lives. The destination—it is just the place in which the journey ends. If life is likened to the journey, death becomes the destination. Who would seek it out?

"And then we took a bus toward Mecca, careful not to violate the sensitivity of anyone. We watched the ceremonies from afar and listened to the stories and accounts from pilgrims who had taken part in all the rituals. And on that night, the night before we left, I asked again of Isabella why it was so necessary to pursue this pilgrimage."

"The destination does not matter, as I said before," she said. "When at the end of life, there is a sense of elevation, changing our perspective and our view. And from this higher sense of clarity, the strangest things will come to mind. While in America, in Pennsylvania, I saw an insect there. For seventeen long years this insect lived within the Earth, beneath the ground. For seventeen long years this *insect* was alive—some sons and daughters do not live so long! And after all that time, a winged creature did emerge to live for only fourteen days above the ground before it mated and it died.

"And so the question begs, 'where was the insect's *life*?' Within the heavens where the insect flew for days and multiplied, or where it grew within the earth for many years? Again, it is the journey, living day to day, that is significant. It teaches us that we must find a singular appreciation in each day we live, must make the most of every opportunity, must learn from each experience.

"This pilgrimage has taught persistence and acceptance, taught we must pursue the things we want with all our energy and yet accept what is not possible. We must enjoy the journey with all passion and accept when it is done. It's not so much the reason or the how or where or why we die that matters in the end, but how we live and we appreciate each day. I kept my promise to my grandfather. Now I am ready to go home."

"I took her home immediately," he said, "because I worried for her health. I brought her home, here to Sevilla. To this very house I brought her home! She wore a purple robe. And oh, Morisco, she was ill—she bled again. She was not well."

Señor was silent for a moment as he sobbed. And I recall I was uncomfortable because this man I hardly knew was pouring out his soul to me. I felt his pain, renewed in memory, could sense the fear and helplessness he felt to know that Isabella would be lost to him a final time. Again, his heart was breaking, and to my surprise, my heart was breaking too. My throat grew tight. I felt a wave of sorrow as a tear trailed down my face.

"Ah, I remember that first night when she was home," the maestro said. "I watched her as she slept and grasped her fragile, trembling, desiccated hand in mine. There I collapsed down to my knees and begged of God. I begged that he would spare her life and tried to offer up my own in place of hers. You seem to sigh, Morisco, but what else has man to bargain but his life, when already he has faith in God? And so I begged my god to let my Isabella live.

"And sometime in the night, when Isabella was delirious, ironically she gave an answer to my prayer. She called my name, 'Antonio!' and then she said to me that 'there are things we must accept in life, while never knowing why.'

"Instead of listening," he said, "I felt resentment in my heart. It was the only time I ever felt a sense of anger toward my god. A child, I asked—and he denied! And with no understanding why! Accept this thing? Accept the loss of Isabella yet again? I could not live without my wife! Why eat or sleep? Why even draw a single breath to know that she would not be at my side? So in this way resentment grew until the sun returned, and with the sun a sense of light within the eyes of Isabella lying there."

"I am not dead yet," sighing, Isabella said, "so why are you, while knowing that I still have life, another day to live and to experience—so why are *you* forlorn and sad? It leads me to believe that you have, in one night, become convinced, like Job, that God has slighted your request and does not hear, when you are feeling sorry only for yourself. Your grief is not for me! You worry for Antonio. O *poor* Antonio! O how *he* will be left alone! And so your grief for me is counterfeit."

"No, you are wrong," Antonio said, "as there is nothing counterfeit about my grief and love and who I am. Perhaps I have been thinking too much of myself, but how could God allow this travesty? How could he take you from me when he knows the beating and the longing in my heart? How could God be so cruel?"

"In that you are mistaken, my Antonio," she said, "As it is God who gives to us our blessings—so he is the giver of good things and does not cause us any harm or pain. God gives us life and health and happiness. Instead, it is our sins within that take our lives away. How could you be so selfish after all the blessings that we have enjoyed? Just think of it. Remember—we have lived adventures that the rest can only dream about. We felt the burning flame of passion in our lives and have experienced the greatest love of all! We shared our lives, and here we are together at this special place and time. *Together!* Please do not forget that we have seen the hand of God! And so instead of sadness, let us greet the day with gratitude. Let us appreciate this gift, another day."

"It is late afternoon," he said. "The sun will disappear and long will be the night. Because of you, I learned to live in light and warmth, and I cannot go back to darkness and the cold. Where you are going, I will go with you. And when you leave, then I will follow close behind unto the grave. I cannot live without my sun."

"But it is not your time," she sighed. "Antonio, my love, please understand that this is not the end for us. The destination lies ahead. And soon the time will come when I will not be able to move forward on my own. The time will come when you will have to carry me, within your heart, your mind and in your memories. In order to arrive together, I will have to be *with* you, and you will have to tell our story to *el Moro*, when he comes."

"*El Moro?*" he exclaimed. "And who is this *el Moro* then? This Moor you speak about?"

"*El Moro*, yes," she said. "And he will come to tell the story of our lives. This Moor will be a relative to me, descended from my grandfather, within that line of blood."

I stopped at once, as I could not believe what he had said.

"*Señor!* Please let me offer my apology," I choked, "Now I *believe* that Isabella told you such a thing, but you have made a terrible mistake! I do regret, but *I* am not the Moor that you are waiting for. No, that would be impossible! There is no way that she could know that I would come today. My coming was an accident of chance! or fate as you would say."

"She knew," he smiled, "yes my beloved Isabella knew this day so long ago. It was her gypsy blood. She knew the very day that you would come. 'In twenty years, in April on the waking moon,' she said, describing your appearance and the very way that I would recognize that you had come."

"No," I argued, unconvinced. "She told you how I would be recognized? And how is this?"

"She said that you would be a Moor in bloodline, dark and intellectual," he said, "and that your quest was for the blood of yet another vine. You traveled here to find your roots, the answer to the mystery of who you are, the bloodline of your ancestry. Before you came to Spain, you searched for family within Morocco, did you not? You tried to find your family there?"

"Well, yes," I said. "That much is true."

"And being disappointed there," he nodded, "Fate, the poet, brought you here to Spain—not to Madrid, where you have history, but to the home of family right here! Here to the Sevillano home where Isabella lived and died! You did not plan to come, but still you *came*! Am I correct?"

Reluctantly, I bowed my head. "I did not plan to come, but it remains that I am not convinced," I answered him.

"The blood and vine that you have sought are here, right here!" he said, "and here your quest is realized. The fire burns. By now you understand why you have come, Morisco. You are home, and you have come for your inheritance, the physical and spiritual—the legacy of Isabella and Antonio."

We sat in silence for some time as I considered so remote a possibility, but he continued as I thought.

"It does not seem so long, but it was twenty years ago tonight when Isabella told me that a Moor, her relative, would come to write the story of our lives, and here you came, upon the very day before, with writing tools and such an eagerness to hear the story through. She knew that you would come. Was she not right?"

He bowed his head and took a breath.

"Perhaps it is coincidence to you, my son," the maestro said, "but Isabella knew. Just *how* you are her relative, she did not say, but she was very sick. I sat beside the bed, her niece and I, for that entire day, and when the evening came, her breath grew faint, ethereal."

"Please be yourself," she said and smiled. "Please always remember me, Antonio, but please again, be who you are, and do what you must do. But swear to me that you will carry me within your memory and in your heart until the day *el Moro* comes. And swear to me that he will write our story down, that he will carry us and share our story with the world for generations yet unborn."

"No need for swearing oaths," he wept. "No force on earth or in the sky could overcome the love I feel for you! For twenty years? If I live for one hundred years, my heart will yearn for only you. And when *el Moro* comes, then I will welcome him as family and swear him to an oath that he will tell our story to the world."

In watching him, it seemed he looked again upon her face. He cried.

"And hearing this, she smiled," he said and bowed his head. "So many years ago, I swore an oath. I made a promise to Fernando that I would not tell what we had done, except within the presence of the angel, Death, or on the day that I would die. Morisco, on today I could reveal the truth to you because today meets both conditions of the oath."

I hardly heard what he had said because my thinking was amiss. *Could it be true?* I thought. For all my life, I've lived within a rational world and had no use for concepts such as faith or fate or destiny, and even God. But something drew me to Sevilla, something inexplicable to me.

At first, I thought I knew why I had come, but I was reconsidering. On two occasions did the airline overbook my flight at Casablanca's busy terminal. I waited idle for two days, and finally, I took a secondary carrier and did not mind that we were laying over in Sevilla in the south of Spain. That was three weeks ago, and since that time, I had not left, and I had never stopped to wonder why. *Could that be destiny or fate?*

"You lost your Isabella on that night?" I asked.

"To lose her? No, that was not possible," he smiled. "But it was on that night that I began to *carry* her. She left a cast behind, but since that time, her memory is colorful and vivid in my thoughts. Her flame still burns. Within my heart and mind I carry her until this day."

"Did she die peacefully?" I asked again.

"The angel caused a gentle breeze to bring her calm," he said, "and then he whispered words of comfort in her ear until the sun was kissing the horizon in the west. And suddenly, she reached for me.

"The day we had was long and glorious!" she said and closed her eyes, and then her breath was gone, transported skyward by the breeze. And weeping, I leaned close and kissed her lips a final time, her face so beautiful in seeming slumber. A glorious sunset, twenty years ago!"

Of course, the maestro seemed to want to weep again, but then it seemed that he was more concerned about the hour—it was almost four a.m.

"Perhaps you have a photo or a likeness I could see?" I asked, "or yet a portrait of your wife, *Señor*, because this claim of blood has made my thoughts aroused and curious."

In order to consider Isabella's claim of family, I knew that I would have to see her face.

The maestro had Luis bring in eleven books of photographs and he encouraged me to take my time, though he seemed anxious all the while. And in these books, I saw a photo of Fernando and I saw the likeness of his father there, his mother and his sisters too. And then I viewed the history of Isabella and Antonio, the many trips that they had undertaken and the images from his description of their life!

And then I saw a single eight-by-ten of Isabella in her youth and sat astonished in my seat. Her face was like my father's mother's face in youth, almost identical in every feature to a photo of his mother that I had at home. And Fátima, the striking beautiful Morisca who was *always* in the other room, the woman who I thought was there in service to Antonio—this Fátima was Isabella's niece, who could have been her mirror-image twin in youth!

And Isabella's grandfather, he gazed into the mirror of my own, or yet the mirror of the father to my grandfather—the eyes, the nose and mouth were similar. I was amazed. Such wild coincidence! I wanted to believe, except my mind was rational. The photos were not proof beyond my doubts. I was intrigued, but I was unconvinced.

"And in the twenty years that she's been gone," I asked, "what have you done? And have you sought *el Moro* out before? Am I the first to hear the story of your life?"

"You are," he said, "as I had sworn an oath and could not speak of my identity before this day. What have I *done*? Now *that* is simple to explain. I have rehearsed to tell this story artfully, the story of my life, the life of me and Isabella, who will always be my wife."

"And did you ever fall in love again?" I interrupted. "Isabella gave you that discretion and permission in the evening that she died."

"To love again? It was not possible," he sighed and seemed to smile, remembering. "When you have had the brightness of the sun, why settle for the twinkling glimmer of the stars and moon?"

"What of Veronica?" I questioned then, "as she was younger than your wife, and in my estimation, she was still in love with you, would always be. So did you see Veronica again?"

"I did!" he said, emphatically. "Her husband died perhaps ten years before today, and being free once more, she sent a letter to my home, inviting me to visit her in Santiago in the north of Spain. Her husband left her wealthy, as Veronica had given him a single heir. In Santiago she had bought a castle—not so large—where she could spend retirement in luxury, but she was lonely there.

"And when I visited, I realized that she was loath to let me quit my stay. She made excuses, she invented causes, almost begging me to still remain, but all this time we had not talked about our past relationship, until one day when we were drinking wine and we were bold.

"'Of course, you know that I have always loved you, my Antonio,' she said and grasped my hand while moving close to me.

"I think you loved my brother," he returned, "and I apologize for my deceit. I needed you and took advantage of a love I knew belonged to him, so I apologize for using you."

"No need!" she laughed. "I knew that I would marry Ferdinand eventually, so I was using you!"

"But when you found out truly who I was," he said, "you tried to take my life."

"I did, and I do not regret," she said. "I was in love with you and passion overtook my senses on that day. When I knew who you were, I realized that I had found the greatest love that I would ever know, though it could never be returned. There was no antidote for Isabella's poison in your blood.

"By killing you, I thought that I could free myself—I thought I could escape the curse, that like venereal disease, is passed to lovers in due course. It is the curse of loving helplessly a person who is helplessly in love with someone else. I passed it to my husband, this while he had passed it to a woman he had spurned to marry me, and who in turn, I know, had crushed another suitor's heart. My husband loved me, but I think he knew I had a secret love for someone else. For you, Antonio, for always you!"

"But you were thinking that you loved Fernando, not Antonio," he disagreed.

"I did not know Fernando with my heart. It was too green and immature. I was a foolish girl who was impressed by him," she said, "and nothing more. But when my heart was ripe and soft and lush, I gave it to Antonio within the many days we spent together, and then at night in bed, and in the morning making love and talking as two children in discovery of life. The time we had was passion-filled. My first and greatest love was you, Antonio Castañeda de Castilla. You have always owned my heart."

"You never loved your husband then?" he asked.

"A marriage of convenience, not of love or will," she said. "A duty to my family, for wealth and reputation in Madrid, but I have learned this axiom: *where there is wealth, then seldom is there passion bound; where there is passion, never will the wealth be found*. Your wife is dead ten years. You are alone, Antonio, and so am I. We loved each other once. Can we now love again?"

She sensed his hesitation and continued on that thought.

"Love me again, Antonio," she said, "it's all I ask of you. And never will I try to be a substitute for Isabella—that would be impossible. I know that you will never have with someone else what you and Isabella had. I know that I am only Leah, who loves you, and true—yet she is Rachel, who you truly love, who died. But I can only be Veronica, and I will love you as no one alive can ever love, with every breath remaining in my body, with every drop of blood within my heart."

"But here I am. I have now almost eighty years from God," he argued then.

She touched his face with gentle hands.

"Here *we* are old," she said, "and here we are together at the pinnacle of life. Please, let us make the most of such a blessed opportunity. And yet I will not beg."

"I have a home and so I cannot stay with you," he said, "as I am waiting for a relative to come. But you are right—the two of us are old, and we together have an opportunity to have reprieve from loneliness and insignificance through words and through the time we spend. Accept that I can only be your friend and nothing more, as I cannot forget my oath or vow. I love my Isabella, even now, and with more passion than I ever have before.

"And so, Veronica and I," he said, "we spent a little time together, moments here and there by chance. The past we shared so long ago had made us relatives of time and cousins of the circumstances that we shared. Sometimes our paths would cross while travelling the world. In vain, she fled from age and loneliness, while I was on eternal quest for blood of vines. The ancient port you drank this night and loved—the port from 1870—Veronica unearthed it from a hidden bunker, buried in the Second Balkan War. Veronica—it was her gift to us this night.

"And on such quests when on ambitious forays in the world, we discovered *viniferous* treasures lost and casks in caches sunken in the treacherous seas. We stole the flask of Dionysus, son of Zeus, and with no thought of impropriety, we drank the nectar that was meant exclusively for gods. As seeming relatives, as ancient friends, we travelled to that place called Napa in America and tasted rarest wines of San Marino and Croatia. We enjoyed five years as such, as merely friends. And when at last Veronica proclaimed that she had finally made peace with frailty and loneliness, her plagues began."

"Unfortunate!" I groaned, "But what can one expect? Our lives are short. And what became of hers?"

"A failure of the kidneys, liver and the pancreas—" he said, "another cancer that in hospitals could not be cured. And oh, the thought of losing yet another relative! I stayed with her while she was in the hospice at her home, while she was dying there.

"And so, one day she said to me, 'Please do not mourn, as you have given me the best experiences of life. Together we had passion in the ring. I stabbed you in the heart and only missed because it oddly rested in another place. We loved and lost and fought our bulls upon the plaza sand. And in the end, we shared the circle ring together. Only now, I know I have been gored and I will die. Please stay with me until the end, Antonio. Please stay and I will tell a secret that I swore an oath to never tell. I see the angel now.'

"And on the day she died, she told me that her son, who lived for forty years, who was her husband's only heir, whose blood eventually would propagate the lines of nobles, dukes and kings— she swore to me that he was my own son, conceived within a night of pleasure, passion and dishonesty, who was my only living heir for years, but she had lost him to a hunting accident. She asked forgiveness for that last deception and she pledged her love to me a final time before the angel guided her away. Yet unexpectedly, she left a sum of wealth to me, which I have never touched.

"And after that, I waited for *el Moro* to arrive, and after five more years, within the afternoon of yesterday, you came. I kept my oath to Isabella, so I am prepared to die today."

"To die?" I gasped. "How could you die today, *Señor*? You are not sick, and neither is your life in jeopardy. You cannot *die!*"

"I will not die in bed," he said, "and with the angel looking on in sympathy. There is no other life worth living, except to be a matador, and there is no other death worth dying, except to die on the arena sand. This afternoon, we will return to *La Maestranza*, where I'll face a bull. Yet if I win, then I will face another bull, and still a third and fourth, if necessary, to achieve my end. I know that I will die today and will not rise from plaza sand.

"I have now eighty-seven years that God has granted me," he sighed, "and I accept that God assigns a time for every thing—a time to come into the world as crying babe and what will follow naturally, a time to die. When you arrived today, I realized there also is a time to know the end has come. So you must swear two oaths to me today, Morisco. Promise me that you will come today into the plaza where I face my final bull, so you can watch me die."

"So I can watch you die?" I nearly screamed. "I only met you yesterday! And from that time, I've learned to think of you as something of a second father in the quest to find the answers I have sought for all my life. I do not have the spleen for such a thing. I do not want to see the end of you!"

"Do not you fret, Morisco," then he said, "remember, mine and every story ends in tragedy, *since all must die*. There is a subtle art or poetry belonging to a life lived to the full. The well-told, well-remembered story is the triumph and the ultimate reward, while sometimes even granting immortality."

"It's inconceivable!" I argued then.

"It is inevitable," he countered, "as I have no one else to watch me die—no other family and no heir to carry me, my flame, away."

"But what of Fernandito?" then I asked. "He saw you as a father, did he not?"

"He died at seventeen, a victim in the ring," he said. "Oh, I am sorry that I did not tell you of his fate, as he is worthy of consideration. Fernandito was a peaceful, pensive boy, unsuited for the passion of the Taurine arts. Fernando's son, he *thought* his way through challenges, but did not feel. So rather than to *feel* the bull, he felt compassion *for* the bull, which is a different thing, and danger in the ring. He died when only seventeen—how young an age! How much is there to tell when one is dead at seventeen? To be a matador is not for every man."

He paused a moment, seeming sad.

"When you are old," he said, "then all that still remains, the only thing of value is the story of your life, your personal account, your history, either rich or lacking worth. Morisco, I entreaty you, if you will tell this story I have shared, then when I die, this house, this property and everything I own is yours, and you will be a wealthy man."

"I do not seek your money or possessions," I protested then. "Already I am wealthy, rich beyond imagination, merely hearing it. So it would be my honor, undeserved, if you would have me share it with the world, if you would trust that I could do so with the passion it deserves. But what am I? I am a simple man who loves to drink the wine and brandy too. I only fear I do not have the eloquence of words to tell it properly."

"I have enormous faith in you," he smiled, "and for that reason, I have waited patiently for twenty years—because I knew that you would come. And Isabella knew, but still she said that I should swear an oath to her, that you would grant us immortality through words.

"So yesterday, I had a lawyer draw up legal documents. When I am gone, then everything you see is yours, and Fátima will be your wife, as Isabella told me was your destiny. She is a niece to us who shares our blood. Will you agree to this arrangement I have made?"

I hesitated naturally, but after thinking for a moment, I agreed, reluctant, nearly overwhelmed.

"This pleases me!" he beamed, "but it is getting late. The story ends upon the plaza sand today, and we have things to do before I face my final bull."

He called Luis, who called the squire, who brought the vestment of a matador, the *traje de luces*, the cape, the cap, the shoes and the assortment of accouterments that squires bring. It took two hours for this man to dress the maestro, who seemed radiant as he feebly struck a pose and practiced moves.

The driver came mere minutes before noon and took us to a building in the business district, where a lawyer had prepared the testament and final will of one *Señor* Fernando Castañeda de Castilla. There were other documents, the purpose meant to transfer wealth.

And after that, the driver took us to the grave of Isabella, where I let the maestro grieve in peace a while and then I joined him on the bench. We sat there quiet for a moment, seeking meaning in our lives by contemplating death, and then he spoke.

"It is late afternoon on April third," he said, "and soon the sun will set."

"But it is only fifteen minutes after one," I differed. "It is not so late."

"My journey has been long," he spoke and smiled, "but there it is—my destination, lying next to her."

At first I was surprised to see the etching on a second marble pedestal, just next to hers. The name: Antonio Castañeda de Castilla! Then I realized that Isabella had been buried in a grave beside Fernando's grave, her former husband, who at his death became Antonio.

"My *son*, Morisco, you... you are my only heir," the maestro said. "So you, my son, will bury me beside my wife, just on the other side. And you will pay someone to switch the pedestals in order to correct the inconsistency and finally erase the fraud of fools we perpetrated long ago on Spain and all the world."

Señor had brought five dozen yellow orchids for his wife and he had brought a flask of cognac for Fernando that he placed upon his brother's grave. And after I returned to wait inside the car, Señor continued on the bench a while. He was explaining something to the seeming air. And then he knelt in prayer, and finally he walked back to the car.

"To *La Maestranza* now, at last!" he told the driver as he smiled. "To face the final bull!"

The stands were full. The crowds were frenzied with excitement, seeking blood of sacrifice beneath the April sun, atonement for the cost of sin. And I was with the maestro as he waited in the *burladero* quietly to know the bull that he would face.

"Ah, *Infierno!*" someone called, "and from the bloodline of *Diablo*, here to fight with Castañeda de Castilla on today!"

At hearing this, I tried to disincline the maestro from this match, while I could not believe *el presidente* would allow a bloody suicide before so many looking on! To think he would permit a man of eighty-seven years to face this dangerous bull! Incredulous, I then protested to officials at the gates, but all to no avail. And after that, I tried to make appeal directly to *el Presidente* at his box, but he heard none of it.

"Today is *Shabbat Shabbaton,*" he said to me, "*Atonement Day.* Fernando—he is Castañeda de Castilla, honored, dear to all of us." *El presidente* sighed, his aspect dour. "I do not like it, but I have the faith to trust he knows what he is doing there."

Yet only then, I realized the maestro had rewarded handsomely *el presidente* for his petulant indulgence in this unannounced and unexpected moment in the ring. And finally, I went to see Antonio himself and begged him to abandon such a waste of life and "an affront to God!"

"But you do not believe in God," he countered as he walked toward certain death, "while I have made my peace with him. And in the end, I know that he will find a way for me, and so my death will be a testament to unbelievers like yourself. If it is possible, then may this cup depart from me—not as I will, but as God wills."

As I continued to complain, I could not understand how no one else was equally offended by this senseless slaughter of so great a man. And when I could protest no more, I sat to watch the death of Antonio Castañeda de Castilla then.

The bull, *Infierno*, came out slow at first. It seemed he knew the bloodline of the matador, and so he moved with caution in each step. He studied quietly Antonio, who wobbled as he stood, and realized the aged man was vulnerable. *Infierno* snorted as his eyes took on a glaze and then he pawed the ground, prepared to charge.

The maestro stood at center of the ring, undaunted, unafraid and ready to engage. With blurring speed, the bull just seemed to disappear while flying toward the trembling target in Antonio's hand. A stunning pass! The maestro showed a flash of what he was before: ¡el Bailarín! The captivated crowds within the stands sang praises to his name: ¡el Bailarín! ¡el Bailarín!

But then the bull squared up again, because he learned the maestro was immobile where the fight was closely-pressed. And then he charged again, and hooking left this time, *Infierno's* horn had almost found its mark. *¡Ah Paletazo!* (or a glancing blow!)

Though it was not enough to cause a serious wound, it knocked the maestro to the ground and crippled him. He coughed a bloody mouthful as he struggled to regain his poise. He slipped and fell, and then he tried to stand again. The spectators at last were horrified. We realized the brutal, gory end was just one savage charge away. I could not watch, and so I tried to close my eyes. I held my breath and waited for the sound of corporal destruction on the sand. And then the bull began to charge.

The maestro was defenseless as he stood there, shaking arms defiantly in front of him, *muleta* and his heavy sword there on the dusty ground. The bull was angry, charging, all with heated blood, with clear intent to kill. And thus was destiny fulfilled. *But no!* For suddenly, as if in fear, the bull dug in its hooves, and desperately it struggled till it stopped in seeming fright and trembled there, its blood abandoning its heart.

And in the dust cloud that its hooves stirred up, a large, ethereal cloud of powder in the air, a cloud that still continued forward even as the bull had stopped, within this cloud of dust I thought I saw the likeness of a man, who stood some fifty feet from head to where his feet were on the earth. His wings were huge, with *azabache* feathers, gleaming in the sun. And in his hand, his right, a sword was drawn and posed to strike, though seconds later, when the cloud had passed, he was no longer there.

At once I wondered if this supernatural man had been a fantasy of my fatigue because I had not slept all night. But then I heard a thunderous and collective gasp from all the people in the stands from all around the plaza seats, a loud and frightened gasp and then a sigh and uttering about this man of such enormous size. It seemed to me that everyone within the plaza witnessed it, beginning with the charging bull.

And on the plaza sand, this cloud of dust, as it continued forward, passing over *Señor* Antonio Castañeda de Castilla standing there, it seemed to take his breath and carry it into the sky. The moment was surreal in altered, slowly-measured time, especially when the maestro smiled with satisfaction in the moment that he looked toward me. And then he bowed a final time before his audience and he collapsed upon the sand.

There was the silence of astonishment, a sense of awe throughout the plaza as the doctor and the priest went to the place he fell and then pronounced him dead. *Infierno*, last of all the bloodline of *Diablo*—they discovered that this bull had also fallen dead, opposing to the end the last of Castañeda de Castilla on the bloodless sand. *El presidente* stood uneasily within his box, with hand on heart, while all around the plaza people spoke of what had passed that afternoon. A *miracle*, the greater part was calling it!

Yet the photographers and those with video equipment, they quickly checked to see if such a spectacle would show on film, but it did not on any camera on that day. The priest explained it was an "act of God," "a call to faith," and such a thing could not be filmed for exploitation purposes.

And in appreciation for the family, for Castañeda de Castilla, flowers rained down from the crowd, carnations, even roses, by the thousands, raining down—so many that the plaza was transformed. And then the men came down to where his body rested at the very center of this floral ring and lifted him. They raised his body high, onto their shoulders, and they carried it away.

I fell upon my knees, astonished, humbled by the words that I had heard from him that day and then the spectacle—I watched him die! My eyes, or yet my mind and heart, sought skyward for the first time in my life, and I accepted what I could not understand. And from that day, the strained and pained prophetic words from that old man are always on my mind, and from that day—*Señor* Antonio Castañeda de Castilla—still his flame I carry in my heart.

Though it was not surprising—as the day went by, I rationalized, and I was less and less convinced of what I saw. It could have been the maestro's shadow there, projected in the dust by slanted background light. But in the seeming angel's hand I saw a sword prepared to strike, *although I knew the maestro's sword was on the ground! ¡Enigma! ¡Paradoja!*

Within the next two days, I did exactly as the maestro had instructed me. The funeral was grand, and people came from many different countries, paying their respects. I had him buried there beside the grave of Isabella, taking special care to switch the pedestals, so that the fraud at last was cured.

And as I wrote this story down, I did consider leaving out the part about the figure of this supernatural man, at risk of sounding foolish, even gullible. Yet what I saw that day has changed my life and my perception of reality. Still I did not believe, nor did I disbelieve, but I had seen and heard such things so that I was inclined to start believing from that moment on.

And when at night I pour the cognac, I will always pour three glasses: one for me, and one for my beloved Antonio—who I will carry all my life until the flame is gone, and then a third for faith itself, as represented by the angel, for those pilgrims who believe.

In irony, I knew *Señor* Antonio for one brief day, from afternoon to afternoon, yet in that span there was a lifetime that we lived together, and perhaps now those who read will live it too. It is the story of Antonio and Isabella, written by a Moor—the story of a lifetime that he shared with me.

In conversation with *Señor* Antonio within the final hour that we spent before he died, I sat with him and asked if I should take up bullfighting, to be like him, to have the life of passion he enjoyed.

"Perhaps that life is not for you," he said. "My son, take up a life of God, as bullfighting alone does not provide a life of passion, wisdom and true love. I never said such words. It is the *living* life that sets apart the matador! Do not be fooled—it is the journey rather than the destination! In the end, the matador will live his life and does not fret. He lives without the fear of death or loss, or broken heart, or disappointment or betrayal. Finally, and most importantly, he does not fear believing, *even in the inconceivable!*"

And so, I have fulfilled my oath with this apology: I have not told this story with the passion it deserves, not with the passion that *Señor* told it to me. Please know that it is but a shadow of the story that I heard.

For Antonio and for Isabella, pass it to a friend or one day read or recommend it to your children as a lesson to inspire and to entertain. And as for me, I finally have found what I was looking for, a starting point, a purpose for my quest for blood of one true vine. Antonio and Isabella changed my life. Thus in this place, this home, my heart has found a counterpoint—as Fátima is at my side—and so I will remain Morisco in Sevilla, where belief has taken root, and on this day, I train to be a matador in life!

¡Olé!

Life Stories: Points to Consider

1) In *Two Matadors*, a story of passion and danger, with conflicts, plot-twists and surprises, the reader undertakes a journey to Sevilla, Spain. At the onset, readers meet the author, Morisco, who admits, "I really hadn't come to tell his story. I came for the wine and *flamenco*." As fate would have it, the story of a lifetime begins. Did you resonate with *Two Matadors*, and what stood out most to you in this story plot?

2) Then the reader meets the old man as he begins to recount a story of love and loss involving two brothers, Antonio and Fernando—identical twins, who are enamored with the same woman, Isabella. Do you think Morisco's account, as told by the old man, accurately describes the life story of Antonio and Isabella? Given various pivotal scenes in the book, which passage or character impressed you or seemed most relevant to the plot?

3) As the narrator, Morisco sets the tone for the book. How are Morisco's opinions and beliefs transformed in the twenty-four hours he spends with Antonio?

4) As mirror-image twins, Antonio and Fernando seem identical, but they are vastly different, and yet over time they literally transform into one another. Fernando accuses Antonio of becoming "the very thing that he fights," while Antonio insists that Fernando is "afraid to live." Which brother wins the argument? In Antonio's place, would you have been true to the vow you made to your brother?

5) Antonio fights and defeats four bulls named in the story: *Pecado* (Sin), *Diablo* (Devil), *Pesar* (Regret), and finally, *Infierno* (Hell), while his brother, Fernando, fights *Muerte* (Death), and Antonio's son, José, fights *Némesis* (Retribution). As readers, did you attach any significance to the names of the bulls and their relevance to the story? If "we *all* fight bulls," and bulls represent life's challenges and defining moments, can you name and describe the bulls in your life story, the circumstances in which you have met or fought with them, and how or if you have defeated them?

6) As the reader indulges in relationship dynamics, Veronica compares a bullfight to "the love affair between a man and a woman." Is this comparison appropriate? In class with Antonio, Fernando's male student likens the matador to "the true believer,

living within a society of unbelievers." What does he mean in this comparison? Do you agree with either assessment?

7) Given we all have a story to tell—if someone were to write your life story, what would be its major themes? Who or what would be the antagonist? Who would be your supporting cast? What would be the major and/or final point of your story?

8) Stories become life legends. Have you ever been profoundly impacted by the life story of someone else, living or dead? How were you changed? Antonio tells Morisco that every life story ends in tragedy (in death). What is the life lesson in Antonio's story? In Isabella's story? In Veronica's story? In Fernando's story? In José's story, in Morisco's story?

9) Relating to symbols in *Two Matadors*, what is the significance of the sun; the stars and moon; the time of day; books; *Shabbat Shabbaton*; the bull; the bullfight; the sword; the plaza; the heart; the vow; the Hand of God; bloodlines; the *pasodoble a flamenco*; the mountain; the flower; the angel; the fireplace log; the pilgrimage; the cicada; the miracle; and the life of a matador.

10) At *Mano de Dios*, Antonio and Isabella stand on the balcony and see the "Hand of God." Have you ever witnessed any evidence of a higher or greater force in your life? Are the lives of Antonio and Isabella better or worse because they are believers? How does believing affect the disposition and the greater arc of a life?

11) Antonio and Isabella have three wedding nights in Morocco. What is Antonio's goal on the first night? How does the second night contrast with the first? What is the significance of the balcony scene on the third night? Contrast the lovemaking of the third night with the couple's week at *Ingles Hotel* in Madrid.

12) Life changing moments occur. Does Morisco really believe what he sees on the plaza sand in the moment before Antonio dies? Have you ever had an experience that could not be explained by any term short of "miraculous?" How was it a life-changing event for you?

If *Two Matadors* has inspired you, please share this story with friends and book clubs around the globe. The author, Marcus McGee, is available for author podcasts and to share personal insights.

order at www.pegasusbooks.net

www.ingramcontent.com/pod-product-compliance
Lightning Source LLC
Chambersburg PA
CBHW022115280326
41933CB00007B/397